Study Guide

for

Slavin

EDUCATIONAL PSYCHOLOGY
THEORY AND PRACTICE

Fifth Edition

prepared by

Catherine E. McCartney
and
Charles E. Alberti

Bemidji State University

Allyn and Bacon
Boston   London   Toronto   Sydney   Tokyo   Singapore

ISBN 0-205-19648-9

Printed in the United States of America

10 9 8 7 6 5 4 3 2 1   01 00 99 98 97 96

CONTENTS

TO THE STUDENT

PURPOSE OF THE STUDY GUIDE

The purpose of this study guide is to reinforce your understanding of the information presented in the text *Educational Psychology: Theory and Practice* by Robert E. Slavin. Both the text and the guide are organized by chapter headings, which are questions focusing on what you should know after you complete your study of the chapters. If you preview the headings for each chapter, study the related text material, and assess your understanding of the content by using this study guide, you should have a firm grasp of the concepts, principles, and theories that make up the field of educational psychology.

ORGANIZATION OF THE CHAPTERS IN THE STUDY GUIDE

CHAPTER OVERVIEW	A brief overview of the concepts presented in the chapter, along with an explanation of how the chapter fits into the rest of the text, is included in this section.
CHAPTER OUTLINE	Chapter headings and subheadings from the text that identify important questions to be answered while reading guide the organization of the outline.
PRACTICE TEST	A series of five to ten questions, worth a total of ten points, is included in this section to assess your understanding of the chapter information. Mastery of the material is reached when you score nine points. Answers to the questions are provided at the end of each chapter.
FOR YOUR INFORMATION	In this section, further study, focusing on the self-check items from the text, is provided if the practice test questions reveal that you have not yet mastered the information.
FOR YOUR ENJOYMENT	In this section, suggestions for enriching your knowledge of chapter information are included.
SELF-ASSESSMENT	This section includes multiple choice, matching, and short essay items covering the main ideas in each chapter. Answers to the questions are included at the end of the study guide.

HOW TO USE THE STUDY GUIDE

1. Preview the headings identified in the text chapter.

2. Read the text chapter while paying close attention to the headings and subheadings.

3. Turn to the *Study Guide* and read the CHAPTER OVERVIEW and the CHAPTER OUTLINE. The points in each should be familiar since they are closely integrated with the text.

4. Recite what you remember from your reading. Use the FOR YOUR ENJOYMENT SECTION to find enrichment, research, or term paper ideas.

5. Use the PRACTICE TEST section to assess your knowledge of the material. If you score less than nine out of ten points, turn to the FOR YOUR INFORMATION section for further study, then complete the SELF-ASSESSMENT items.

1
EDUCATIONAL PSYCHOLOGY:
A FOUNDATION FOR TEACHING

CHAPTER OVERVIEW

The purpose of this chapter is to provide you with a foundation for understanding effective teaching by using research from the field of educational psychology. Some of the things already learned from studies in educational psychology are listed below.

Educational psychology describes good teachers as those who possess subject matter knowledge and pedagogical knowledge (teaching "know how") that they combine with common sense to make sound decisions about classroom events.

Educational psychology has taught us that good teachers use quantitative and qualitative research findings that describe teaching effectiveness to guide their instruction.

CHAPTER OUTLINE

I. WHAT MAKES A GOOD TEACHER?
    A. Knowing the Subject Matter
    B. Mastering the Teaching Skills
    C. Can Good Teaching be Taught?
    D. Teaching as Critical Thinking
    E. Teachers as Self-Regulated Learners

II. WHAT IS THE ROLE OF RESEARCH IN EDUCATIONAL PSYCHOLOGY?
    A. Goals of Research in Educational Psychology
    B. The Value of Research in Educational Psychology
    C. Teaching as Decision Making
    D. Research + Common Sense = Effective Teaching

III. WHAT RESEARCH METHODS ARE USED IN EDUCATIONAL PSYCHOLOGY?
    A. Experiments
    B. Correlational Studies
    C. Descriptive Research

PRACTICE TEST

DIRECTIONS: Each chapter heading from the text listed below is followed by a series of related questions worth a total of ten points. Respond to each question, check your answers with those found at the end of the study guide chapter, then determine your score. Consider nine points per heading to be mastery.

For those headings on which you do not score at least nine points, turn to the FOR YOUR INFORMATION section of the study guide for corrective instruction. For those headings on which you do score at least nine points, turn to the FOR YOUR ENJOYMENT section of the study guide for enrichment activities.

I. WHAT MAKES A GOOD TEACHER?

True or False

1. (1 point) _____ According to your text author, personal characteristics such as leadership, humor, and enthusiasm are only part of what makes someone an effective teacher.

2. (1 point) _____ The connection between what the teacher wants students to know and what the students actually learn is called *pedagogy*.

3. (1 point) _____ Effective teaching is a matter of one person with more knowledge transmitting that knowledge to someone with less.

Multiple Choice

4. (1 point) _____ A teacher who sees situations clearly, identifies potential problems, and explores possible solutions

    A. is a self-regulated learner.
    B. possesses subject matter knowledge.
    C. is a critical thinker.
    D. is an expert teacher.

5. (1 point) _____ Teachers who take responsibility for their own knowledge and skills, set learning goals, motivate themselves to learn, then monitor and assess what they have learned are called

    A. master teachers.
    B. critical thinkers.
    C. decision makers.
    D. self-regulated learners.

Short Answer/Essay

6. (3 points) List three components of good teaching.

_____

_____

_____

7. (2 points) Explain how good teaching can be taught.

_____

_____

_____

_____

II. WHAT IS THE ROLE OF RESEARCH IN EDUCATIONAL PSYCHOLOGY?

True or False

8. (1 point) _____ A goal of educational psychology research is to carefully examine questions about teaching and learning using objective methods.

9. (1 point) _____ Principles and theories from educational psychology research are interpreted in similar ways by different individuals, making progress in the field steady and evenly paced.

10. (3 points)

Matching

_____ set of related relationships that explain broad aspects of an area of study   A. laws

_____ ideas that have been thoroughly tested and found to apply to a wide variety of situations   B. principles   C. theories

_____ an explanation of the relationship between factors

Multiple choice

11. (1 point) _____ Which of the following ideas about teaching can be supported by educational psychology research?

A. Schools that spend more money per pupil will produce higher achieving students than schools that spend less.
B. If students are assigned to classes according to their ability, the resulting narrow range of abilities in a class will let the teacher adapt the instruction to the students' needs, resulting in higher achievement.
C. Scolding students in order to improve behavior may work for many, but for some it is a reward.
D. Competition among students, not cooperation, is most effective in terms of achievement.

12. (1 point) _____ When you combine objective research with common sense, the result is

A. effective teaching.
B. self-regulated learning.
C. inconsistent student achievement.
D. decreased quality in decision making.

13. (1 point) _____ Which of the following statements regarding teacher decision making is false?

A. Sound decision making depends on the situation within which a problem arises.
B. Sound decision making depends on the objectives the teacher has in mind.
C. It is necessary to combine principles and theories from educational psychology with common sense when making decisions.
D. Principles and theories from educational psychology can be considered free of context.

14. (2 points)

Short Answer/Essay

List two ways you can use critical thinking when making decisions about teaching.

_____

_____

III. WHAT RESEARCH METHODS ARE USED IN EDUCATIONAL PSYCHOLOGY?

Matching

15. (3 points) _____ examples of this type of research include surveys, interviews, or observations which take place in a social setting

             _____ type of research where special treatments are created and their effects are analyzed

             _____ type of research where relationships between variables, as they naturally occur, are analyzed

A. experimental research

B. correlational research

C. descriptive research

Multiple Choice

16. (1 point) _____ One advantage to this type of experimental research is that there is a high degree of control over all factors involved. One disadvantage is that the artificial conditions under which the experiment is conducted may yield results that have little real-life relevance. What type of research is being described in the above statements?

A. laboratory experiment
B. randomized-field experiment
C. single-case experiment

17. (1 point) _____ A special education teacher collects data on the number of times a student's hand-raising behavior occurs over a period of several days after a new assertiveness program has been implemented. What type of research is being described in this scenario?

A. laboratory experiment
B. randomized-field experiment
C. single-case experiment

18. (1 point) _____ Which of the following experimental research types attempts to control all factors except those created by the treatment while simultaneously remaining relevant to real life?

A. laboratory experiment
B. randomized-field experiment
C. single-case experiment

19. (1 point) _____ A researcher found that students who scored high on a test of reading achievement also scored high on a self-esteem inventory. The researcher can say that reading achievement and self-esteem are

    A. negatively correlated.
    B. positively correlated.
    C. uncorrelated.

20. (1 point) _____ Which of the following examples depicts a negative correlation?

    A. Students who studied for the greatest length of time prior to a math test received the highest scores.
    B. The amount of time students studied for a math test was unrelated to the scores they received.
    C. Students who were absent the least prior to a math test received the highest scores.

Short Answer/Essay

21. (2 points) Explain the difference between causal and correlation relationships.

_____

_____

_____

_____

SCORING	POINTS NEEDED FOR MASTERY	POINTS RECEIVED
I. WHAT MAKES A GOOD TEACHER?	9	_____
II. WHAT IS THE ROLE OF RESEARCH IN EDUCATIONAL PSYCHOLOGY?	9	_____
III. WHAT RESEARCH METHODS ARE USED IN EDUCATIONAL PSYCHOLOGY?	9	_____

FOR YOUR INFORMATION

This section of the study guide includes suggestions for further study of the information you have not yet mastered. You will find information on: 1) typical responses to the SELF-CHECK item(s) from the text; and 2) key concepts, principles, and theories addressed in the text chapter.

I. WHAT MAKES A GOOD TEACHER?

1. SELF-CHECK ITEM: Reassess the chapter opening scenario. In terms of the concepts introduced in this section, what qualities identify Leah as a good teacher?

TYPICAL RESPONSE: What qualities identify Leah as a good teacher?

Qualities of a Good Teacher	Qualities of Leah Washington
motivates students	Leah says, "I read students funny and intriguing stories . . . to arouse their curiosity."
assesses prior knowledge	Leah says, "I adapt to the needs of each learner by conferencing with students and helping them with specific problems."
communicates effectively	Leah "gradually introduced 'mini-lessons' to help [students] become better authors."
takes into account the characteristics of the learner	Leah says, "I adapt to students' developmental level and cultural style by encouraging them to write about things that matter to them."
assesses learning outcomes	Leah says, "Everybody gets an 'A' on his or her composition, but only when it meets a high standard, which may take many drafts."
reviews information	Leah "[has] 'writing celebrations' in which students read their finished compositions to the class for applause and comment."

2. KEY CONCEPTS, PRINCIPLES, AND THEORIES

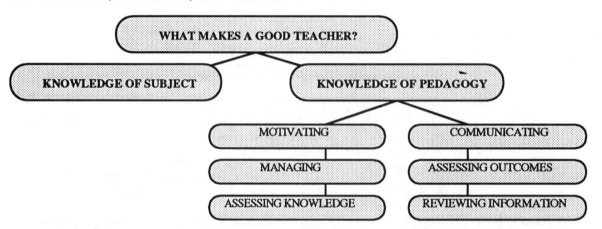

II. WHAT IS THE ROLE OF RESEARCH IN EDUCATIONAL PSYCHOLOGY?

1. SELF-CHECK ITEM: Suggest some common sense ways in which the following findings from educational psychology research might help you to be more effective as a teacher.

- Children are generally not capable of formal logic and hypothetical reasoning before age 11.
- Students better observe rules they have helped to set and are better motivated to learn topics they have helped to select.
- Misbehavior for which attention is the reward will diminish if attention is not given.

What does research tell us about effective teaching?

TYPICAL RESPONSE: Suggest some common sense ways in which the findings from educational psychology research might help you to be more effective as a teacher.

Theory	Practice
Children do not think logically nor hypothetically.	Ground lessons in the concrete, the here-and-now, and the familiar.
Students prefer to be a part of the decision making process for rules and subject content.	Allow students to create class rules through brainstorming, prioritizing, and discussing. Allow students to express their interest in the content by individualizing projects, research papers, or other assignments.
Students misbehave for attention.	Ignore or minimize attention given to inappropriate behaviors while maximizing attention given to appropriate behaviors.

TYPICAL RESPONSE: What does research tell us about effective teaching?

Research tells us that effective teaching depends on more than theory -- it also depends on context. Whether or not a problem can be solved, objectives can be met, or learning can occur depends on the teacher, the learner, and the situation. Research tells us that common sense plays an important role in teaching effectiveness.

2. KEY CONCEPTS, PRINCIPLES, AND THEORIES

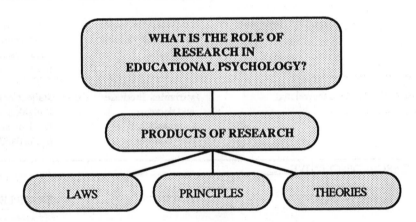

III. WHAT RESEARCH METHODS ARE USED IN EDUCATIONAL PSYCHOLOGY?

1. SELF-CHECK ITEM: Construct a comparison chart with the columns headed Experimental, Correlation, and Descriptive. Enter information in the following categories: goals of research, forms studies take, kinds of findings, examples. Then write a paragraph explaining why correlations must not be confused with causes.

TYPICAL RESPONSE: Construct a comparison chart with the columns headed Experimental, Correlation, and Descriptive.

TYPE OF RESEARCH: EXPERIMENTAL

GOALS	FORMS	FINDINGS	EXAMPLES FROM TEXT
test effectiveness of treatment	laboratory	internally valid	rewards can diminish interest in an activity
	randomized-field	externally valid	MMP was more effective than traditional methods of teaching math
	single-case	measures frequently observed behaviors	"Good Behavior Game"

TYPE OF RESEARCH: CORRELATIONAL

GOALS	FORMS	FINDINGS	EXAMPLES FROM TEXT
look for relationships between variables	positive correlation	high scores for one variable are related to high scores for another	+ correlation between reading and math achievement
	negative correlation	one variable increases as another variable decreases	- correlation between math achievement and days absent from instruction
	uncorrelated	variables increase and decrease independently of one another	student achievement in Poughkeepsie, NY and level of student motivation in Portland, OR

TYPE OF RESEARCH: DESCRIPTIVE

GOALS	FORMS	FINDINGS	EXAMPLES
seeks to describe something of interest	survey interviews ethnography	observations of what exists naturally in the environment	describe meaning and consequence of desegregation at three high schools

TYPICAL RESPONSE: Write a paragraph explaining why correlations must not be confused with causes.

Correlational research and experimental research differ in that correlational research describes relationships between variables while experimental research looks for causes and effects. Saying that two variables are related, as with correlational research, does not imply that one caused the other, only that they are somehow related.

2. KEY CONCEPTS, PRINCIPLES, AND THEORIES

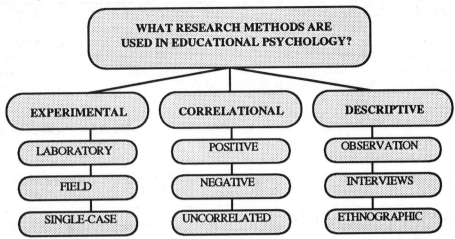

FOR YOUR ENJOYMENT

This section of the study guide includes suggestions for enriching your understanding of a chapter heading you have mastered. You will find information on activities related to the heading and suggestions for research papers, interviews, or presentations.

I. WHAT MAKES A GOOD TEACHER?

1. Make a list of positive personal characteristics that you believe you possess.
   A. For each characteristic, determine if it is essential for good teaching.
   B. Rank order the characteristics from most essential to least essential.
   C. Ask administrators, teachers, and students to rank order your list of characteristics in the same manner as described above. Compare and discuss your lists with others.

2. For a research topic, review the literature on expertise development and its application to teaching.

II. WHAT IS THE ROLE OF RESEARCH IN EDUCATIONAL PSYCHOLOGY?

1. Review some educational psychology and education journals. Make a list of the type of questions asked by the researchers.

2. Interview teachers about their methods of making educational decisions. Do they use formal or informal research methods?

3. For a research topic, review the literature on teachers as researchers.

III. WHAT RESEARCH METHODS ARE USED IN EDUCATIONAL PSYCHOLOGY?

1. Do teachers call on students with different degrees of frequency? Observe in a classroom for at least one hour. Using a seating chart, keep track of the students who are called on by the teacher. From your data, answer the following questions:
   A. If you divide the room into quadrants, does any one quadrant dominate in the number of times students are called on by the teacher? Can you identify any other patterns?
   B. If you identify the gender of each student, are males or females called on more often?

2. Identify a question related to educational psychology that you would like to have answered. Design a research study to address your question. Include a statement of the problem as well as the design and procedure you will use to study the question.

3. Review some educational psychology and education journals. What type of research designs are used?

CHAPTER ONE: SELF-ASSESSMENT

DIRECTIONS: Below are questions related to the main ideas presented in the chapter. Correct answers or typical responses can be found at the end of the study guide.

1.   Write a paragraph that begins with the following topic sentence: Effective teaching requires critical thinking.

2.   A product of educational psychology research that explains relationships between factors that influence behavior is called a

    A. fact.
    B. principle.
    C. theory.
    D. law.

3.   Which of the following pairs correctly matches a type of research to an advantage that it offers?

    A. laboratory experiment; has high internal validity
    B. randomized field experiment; exercises rigorous control
    C. descriptive study; shows relationships between variables
    D. single-case experiment; involves infrequent assessment

4.   Match the following types of experiment with the situations they illustrate (situation may be used more than once or not at all).

    _____ randomized field experiment

    _____ descriptive research

    _____ laboratory experiment

    _____ correlational study

    A. observing and noting how preschoolers play

    B. recording the number of times a student misbehaves, before and after the use of a special reinforcement program

    C. determining the relationship between reading ability and math achievement

    D. evaluating a new teaching technique for several months under typical classroom conditions

    E. evaluating a new teaching technique for a short period of time under highly controlled conditions.

5.   Students in Ms. Jameson's class receive a check mark for each day they fail to turn in homework. How is the number of check marks received by midterm likely to correlate with midterm test scores in that class?

    A. positively
    B. negatively
    C. no correlation

6. Studies in educational psychology that offer the greatest internal validity are

   A. randomized field experiments.
   B. laboratory experiments.
   C. ethnographies.
   D. correlational studies.

7. In a hypothetical schoolwide correlational study, the relationship between the numbers of days a student was absent during a marking period to the next was shown on the average to have a negative correlation. This negative correlation would mean that

   A. absenteeism causes lower class rankings.
   B. the study does not have external validity.
   C. class rankings tend to rise as attendance increases.
   D. class rank decreases absenteeism.

8. Refer to the scenario about Ellen Mathis and Leah Washington that begins this chapter. Ellen could not believe that the theoretical ideas of her educational psychology class could be applied so directly to her third grade creative writing class. How might theories of educational psychology apply to reading, science, social studies, or special education?

9. What is the difference between a field based study and a laboratory study? What is an advantage and disadvantage of each?

PRACTICE TEST ANSWERS

1. True; Leadership, humor, and enthusiasm are important personal characteristics of teachers. So are warmth, planning, hard work, self-discipline, a contagious love of learning, speaking ability, and a variety of other characteristics.

2. True; Pedagogy is the link between what the teacher wants students to learn and what students actually learn.

3. False; Effective teaching is not a simple matter of one person with more knowledge transmitting that knowledge to another.

4. C; Effective teaching requires critical thinking: seeing situations clearly, identifying problems, and exploring possible solutions.

5. D; Self-regulated learners take responsibility for their knowledge and skills, set learning goals, motivate themselves to learn, monitor their own progress, assess their own mastery, and redirect the course of their own learning.

6. Components of good teaching include motivating students, managing classrooms, assessing prior knowledge, communicating, and reviewing information.

7. Good teaching can be taught in two ways. First, teach the principles of effective teaching and, second, teach how to apply the principles.

8. True; The goal of research in educational psychology is to carefully examine obvious as well as less obvious questions, using objective methods to test ideas about the factors that contribute to learning.

9. False; The same facts and principles may be interpreted in different ways by different theorists, making progress slow and uneven.

10. C, A, B; Theories are sets of related principles and laws that explain broad aspects of learning. Laws are simply principles that have been thoroughly tested and found to apply to a wide variety of situations. Principles explain relationships between factors.

11. C; Many teachers believe that scolding students for misbehavior will improve student behavior. While this is true for many students, for others scolding may be a reward for misbehavior and actually increase it.

12. A; Research + Common Sense = Effective Teaching.

13. D; Making the right decision depends on the situation within which the problem arises, the objectives the teacher has in mind, and a combination of research and common sense.

14. Critical thinking is used in teaching when situations are clearly seen, problems are identified, and possible solutions are explored.

15. C, A, B; Descriptive research includes surveys, interviews, or observations in a social setting. Experimental research creates special treatments and analyzes the effects. Correlational research looks at relationships between variables.

16. A; Laboratory experiments permit researchers to exert a high degree of control over all factors involved in the study, but doing so makes it highly artificial.

17. C; Single-case experiments demonstrate the effects of a treatment on one person or one group by comparing behavior before, during, and after treatment.

18. B; Randomized-field experiments demonstrate the effects of a treatment under realistic conditions.

19. B; A positive correlation shows that as one set of variables increases (reading achievement scores), so does another set (self-esteem scores).

20. C; A negative correlation shows that as one set of variables increases (test scores), the other set decreases (absences).

21. Causal research demonstrates cause and effect relationships while correlational research demonstrates relationships between variables.

2
THEORIES OF DEVELOPMENT

CHAPTER OVERVIEW

The purpose of both this and the next chapter is to discuss major theorists and theories of human development -- the ways in which people grow, adapt, and change during their lifetimes. Some of the major theorists' ideas about cognitive, personal/social, and moral development appear below.

Human development is the study of growth, adaptations, and changes that occur in cognition over time. Jean Piaget and Lev Vygotsky studied differences in individuals' thinking and language development.

Human development is the study of growth, adaptations, and changes that occur in personality and social relationships as individuals mature. Erik Erikson devised a lifespan approach to personal/social development.

Human development is the study of growth, adaptations, and changes that occur in moral behavior over time. Jean Piaget, Lawrence Kohlberg, and Martin Hoffman studied how development affected moral reasoning.

CHAPTER OUTLINE

I. WHAT ARE SOME VIEWS OF HUMAN DEVELOPMENT?
   A. Aspects of Development
   B. Issues of Development

II. HOW DID PIAGET VIEW COGNITIVE DEVELOPMENT?
   A. How Development Occurs
   B. Assimilation and Accommodation
   C. Piaget's Stages of Development

III. HOW IS PIAGET'S WORK VIEWED TODAY?
   A. Criticisms and Revisions of Piaget's Theory
   B. Educational Implications of Piaget's Theory
   C. Neo-Piagetian and Constructivist Views of Development

IV. HOW DID VYGOTSKY VIEW COGNITIVE DEVELOPMENT?
   A. How Development Occurs
   B. Applications of Vygotskian Theory in Teaching

V. HOW DID ERIKSON VIEW PERSONAL AND SOCIAL DEVELOPMENT?
   A. Stages of Psychosocial Development
   B. Implications and Criticisms of Erikson's Theory

VI. WHAT ARE SOME THEORIES OF MORAL DEVELOPMENT?
   A. Piaget's Theory of Moral Development
   B. Kohlberg's Stages of Moral Reasoning
   C. Hoffman's Development of Moral Behavior

PRACTICE TEST

DIRECTIONS: Each chapter heading from the text listed below is followed by a series of related questions worth a total of ten points. Respond to each question, check your answers with those found at the end of the study guide chapter, then determine your score. Consider nine points per heading to be mastery.

For those headings on which you do not score at least nine points, turn to the FOR YOUR INFORMATION section of the study guide for corrective instruction. For those headings on which you do score at least nine points, turn to the FOR YOUR ENJOYMENT section of the study guide for enrichment activities.

I. WHAT ARE SOME VIEWS OF HUMAN DEVELOPMENT?

True or False

1. (1 point) _____ One of the first requirements of effective teaching is that all students be treated equally, regardless of developmental characteristics.

2. (1 point) _____ Development refers to the changes in physical, personal, social, cognitive, and moral characteristics that occur over the lifespan.

3. (1 point) _____ Children are like miniature adults; their thinking is qualitatively the same as adults' thinking.

Matching

4. (3 points) _____ major developmental theorist who studied cognition

             _____ major developmental theorists who studied moral reasoning

             _____ major developmental theorist who studied personal growth and social relationships

A. Erik Erikson

B. Lawrence Kohlberg

C. Jean Piaget

Short Answer/Essay

5. (2 points) Define and give an example of a continuous theory of development.

_____

_____

6. (2 points) Define and give an example of a discontinuous theory of development.

_____

_____

II. HOW DID PIAGET VIEW COGNITIVE DEVELOPMENT?

Sentence Completion

7. (1 point) _____ Mental patterns that guide thinking and behavior are called ___.

8. (1 point) _____ The process of incorporating new information into existing schemes is called ___.

9. (1 point) _____ The process of modifying existing schemes so that new knowledge can be understood is called ___.

Matching

10. (4 points) _____ inferred reality -- the ability to see things in context -- is a characteristic of an individual who is at this stage

A. sensorimotor stage

B. preoperational stage

_____ hypothetical thought -- the ability to deal with possibilities -- is a characteristic of of an individual who is at this stage

C. concrete operational stage

_____ object permanence -- knowing that an object exists when it is out of sight -- is a characteristic of an individual who is at the end of this stage

D. formal operational stage

_____ egocentric behavior -- believing that everyone shares his or her beliefs -- is a characteristic of an individual who is at this stage

Multiple Choice

11. (1 point) _____ Which of the following is an example of Piaget's *conservation*?

A. A student is able to explain why the amount of water poured from a short, wide beaker into a tall, narrow beaker remains constant.
B. A student can select one choice from a variety of alternatives in order to form a hypothesis.
C. A student who used to call all small animals "kitty" can now discriminate between a cat and a skunk.
D. A student can place 10 sticks of various lengths in order from shortest to tallest.

12. (1 point) _____ At the end of Piaget's concrete operational stage, a child is capable of all of the following tasks EXCEPT

A. class inclusion.
B. transitivity.
C. decentration.
D. testing hypotheses.

13. (1 point) _____ The abilities that make up formal operational thought are critical to learning which of the following cognitive tasks?

A. conservation
B. higher-order thinking skills
C. assimilation and accommodation
D. equilibration

III. HOW IS PIAGET'S WORK VIEWED TODAY?

True or False

14. (1 point) _____ Piaget believed that developmental stages are fixed -- that certain cognitive tasks cannot be completed until the individual is developmentally ready.

15. (1 point) _____ A strength of Piaget's theory is that he considers culture and context in relationship to development.

16. (1 point) _____ Neo-Piagetians have found that Piaget's beliefs about children's egocentrism -- seeing only their own point of view -- remains accurate even when familiar tasks and age-appropriate language are used in testing.

Multiple Choice

17. (1 point) _____ Which of the following best describes the concept of "developmentally appropriate education?"

A. It focuses on active teacher and passive student interactions.
B. It is product-oriented.
C. It is suitable for students in terms of their development needs.
D. It focuses on group, rather than individual, achievement.

18. (1 point) _____ The view of cognitive development as a process in which children actively build systems of meaning and understandings of reality through experience and interaction, is known as

A. comparative human cognition.
B. constructivism.
C. "the American question."
D. a rules-assessment approach.

19. (1 point) _____ Which of the following represents an example of a constructivist view of development?

A. ecological systems theory
B. development precedes learning
C. information processing approach
D. rules systems theory

Short Answer/Essay

20. (4 points) List four educational implications of Piaget's theory of cognitive development.

_____

_____

_____

_____

IV. HOW DID VYGOTSKY VIEW COGNITIVE DEVELOPMENT?

True or False

21. (1 point) _____ One important contribution of Vygotsky's theory is that it emphasizes the sociocultural nature of learning.

22. (1 point) _____ According to Vygotsky, mental functioning exists within the individual before it exists in conservation and collaboration.

Sentence Completion

23. (1 point) _____ A term used to describe a developmental phase of learning in which a child will fail at a task if attempted independently, but not if he or she is given support, is called ___.

24. (1 point) _____ A mechanism for turning shared knowledge into personal knowledge is ___.

25. (1 point) _____ Providing a child with support during the early stages of learning and then encouraging him or her to take on greater responsibility as the task becomes more familiar is known as ___.

26. (1 point) _____ A type of assessment where the teacher gives hints and prompts at different levels of complexity is called ___ assessment.

Short Answer/Essay

27. (4 points) List two major educational implications of Vygotsky's theory and give an example of each.

_____

_____

_____

_____

V. HOW DID ERIKSON VIEW PERSONAL AND SOCIAL DEVELOPMENT?

True or False

28. (1 point) _____ Erikson proposed that individuals pass through eight psychosocial stages with a crisis to be resolved at each stage.

29. (1 point) _____ Most people resolve developmental crises as they pass through the psychosocial stages, but some do not and end up dealing with them later in life.

30. (1 point) _____ Erikson's theory de-emphasizes the role of the environment, both in causing a crisis and in determining how it will be resolved.

31. (4 points) _____ *Matching*
stage where "Who am I?"
becomes important

            _____ stage where the focus is
"I am what I learn"

            _____ stage of exploration of the
physical and social environment

            _____ stage dedicated to finding oneself
in another

A. initiative vs. guilt

B. industry vs. inferiority

C. identity vs. role confusion

D. intimacy vs. isolation

Short Answer/Essay

32. (3 points)   List an educational experience that will help to develop: 1) initiative;
2) industry; and 3) identity.

_____

_____

_____

VI. WHAT ARE SOME THEORIES OF MORAL DEVELOPMENT?

Sentence Completion

33. (1 point) _____ According to Piaget, a type of moral reasoning in which a child believes that
rules are fixed and unchangeable is called __.

34. (1 point) _____ According to Piaget, a type of moral reasoning in which a child considers a
transgressor's intentions is called __.

35. (1 point) _____ A structured moral situation developed by Kohlberg is known as a(an) __.

Matching

36. (3 points) _____ level of moral reasoning in which
individuals obey authority figures
to avoid punishment

            _____ level of moral reasoning in which
individuals use ethical principles to
guide moral behavior

            _____ level of moral reasoning in which
individuals follow social rules

A. preconventional level

B. conventional level

C. postconventional level

Multiple Choice

37. (1 point) _____ According to Kohlberg, individuals progress from stage to stage by

   A. interacting with those whose moral reasoning is at a higher level.
   B. resolving critical and conflicting psychosocial issues.
   C. exhibiting socially acceptable behavior.
   D. seeking approval and avoiding punishment.

38. (1 point) _____ Martin Hoffman's theory of moral development compliments the work of Piaget and Kohlberg by acknowledging

   A. other experts in the field.
   B. the role of cognition in explaining moral behavior.
   C. that guilt is not a motivating factor.
   D. that students should essentially be left to develop on their own.

Short Answer/Essay

39. (2 points) List two limitations of Kohlberg's theory of moral development.

_____

_____

SCORING	POINTS NEEDED FOR MASTERY	POINTS RECEIVED
I. WHAT ARE SOME VIEWS OF HUMAN DEVELOPMENT?	9	_____
II. HOW DID PIAGET VIEW HUMAN DEVELOPMENT?	9	_____
III. HOW IS PIAGET'S WORK VIEWED TODAY?	9	_____
IV. HOW DID VYGOTSKY VIEW COGNITIVE DEVELOPMENT?	9	_____
V. HOW DID ERIKSON VIEW PERSONAL AND DEVELOPMENT?	9	_____
VI. WHAT ARE SOME THEORIES OF MORAL DEVELOPMENT?	9	_____

FOR YOUR INFORMATION

This section of the study guide includes suggestions for further study of the information you have not yet mastered. You will find information on: 1) typical responses to the SELF-CHECK item(s) from the text; and 2) key concepts, principles, and theories addressed.

I. WHAT ARE SOME VIEWS OF HUMAN DEVELOPMENT?

1. SELF-CHECK ITEM: Begin a four-column comparison chart listing Piaget, Vygotsky, Erikson, and Kohlberg, each at the head of a column. Identify the theory each proposed, the type of development involved, and whether the theory is continuous or discontinuous. After you finish reading the chapter, explain the three opening vignettes in terms of the theories and concepts presented in the chapter.

TYPICAL RESPONSE: Begin a comparison chart of Piaget, Vygotsky, Erikson, and Kohlberg.

	PIAGET	VYGOTSKY	ERIKSON	KOHLBERG
THEORY PROPOSED	development depends on manipulation and active interaction with the environment	development depends on the sociocultural nature of learning	development depends on the resolution of psychosocial crises	development depends on reasoning about rules that govern behavior
TYPE	cognitive (discontinuous)	cognitive (discontinuous)	personal/social (discontinuous)	moral (discontinuous)

TYPICAL RESPONSE: Explain the opening vignettes in terms of theories and concepts presented.

Mr. Jones: The teacher's students are preoperational (Piaget's second stage of cognitive development). This means that the children cannot reverse operations, focus on more that one aspect of a problem at a time, or consider another point of view.

Ms. Quintera: Ms. Quintera's student, Frank, is working on resolving issues of identity (Erikson's fourth stage of psychosocial development) which involve breaking away from parents and from those who exhibit "parental" behaviors -- teachers.

Ms. Lewis: Ms. Lewis' students are in Piaget's stage of heteronomous morality or Kohlberg's preconventional level of moral development where rules are absolute and punishment is consistent, regardless of intent.

2. KEY CONCEPTS, PRINCIPLES, AND THEORIES

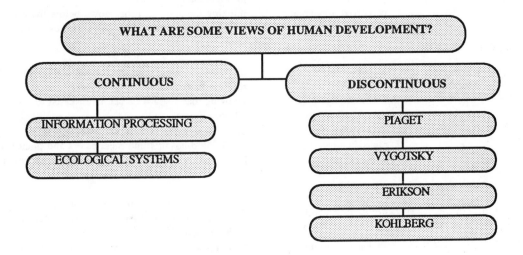

II. HOW DID PIAGET VIEW COGNITIVE DEVELOPMENT?

1. SELF-CHECK ITEM: Think of an original example from your own experience or observations for each of the following phenomena as described by Piaget: scheme, assimilation, accommodation, equilibration. Add Piaget's four stages of development to the comparison chart you started in the first SELF-CHECK. Then, classify the following phenomena or capabilities in terms of Piaget's stages. At what stage is each one achieved? Give an example of each one.

TYPICAL RESPONSE: Think of an original example of scheme, assimilation, accommodation, and equilibration.

Piagetian Term	Example
scheme	Organizing your understanding of trees into coniferous and deciduous.
assimilation	A child I know believed the earth is flat because the horizon is flat. When told that the earth is round, she assimilated it to mean round and flat -- like a disk.
accommodation	My niece just learned that hymns are not "boys' songs" (hims).
equilibration	Trying to remember someone's name when I can't (disequilibration), then suddenly remembering it (equilibration).

TYPICAL RESPONSE: Add Piaget's stages of development and tasks to be accomplished at each stage to your chart.

PIAGET STAGE	TASKS	EXAMPLES
sensorimotor	object permanence	looking for a toy when it is out of sight
	reflexes	placing your finger in the palm of an infant's hand and the infant grasping it
	use of symbols	using words to represent thought ("Mama")
	goal direction	pulling on a blanket holding a toy that is out of reach
preoperational	centration	considering height, but not width, when solving a problem that involves both
	perceived appearances	thinking the sun sets (goes down below the earth)
	egocentrism	thinking that farmers have cows so they can play with them
concrete operational	inferred reality	knowing the illusion of the sun setting is caused by the rotation of the earth
	reversibility	knowing that 7 + 5 = 12 can be reversed to show that 12 - 5 = 7
	inversion	knowing that 1/2 is different from 2/1
	classification	arranging dinosaurs into meat eaters and plant eaters
	conservation	knowing that the volume of a liquid poured from one container to another remains constant
formal operational	use of logic	reasoning through an analytic problem; Tim is taller than Dave, Dave is taller than Steve, therefore, Tim is taller than Steve
	abstract thinking	thinking what it would have been like had Germany won WWII

22

2. KEY CONCEPTS, PRINCIPLES, AND THEORIES

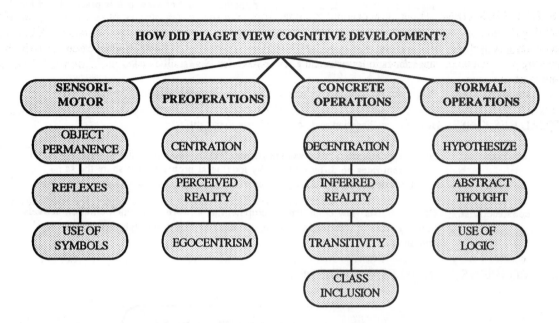

III. HOW IS PIAGET'S WORK VIEWED TODAY?

1. SELF-CHECK ITEM: List four general teaching implications that reflect Piagetian principles. Describe in detail an example of a teaching strategy that applies Piagetian concepts in the classroom. Briefly summarize the arguments against Piaget's theory of cognitive development. How do neo-Piagetian and constructivist views of development differ?

TYPICAL RESPONSE: List four general teaching implications that reflect Piagetian principles.

> Teaching Implications:
> Focus on the process of children's thinking, not just its products.
> Recognize the crucial role of children's self-initiated, active involvement in learning activities.
> De-emphasize practices aimed at making children adult-like in their thinking.
> Accept individual differences in developmental progress.

TYPICAL RESPONSE: Describe in detail a teaching strategy that applies Piagetian concepts in the classroom.

> Classroom Strategy: Discovery
> Present a puzzling situation well matched to the learner's developmental stage.
> Elicit student responses and ask for justification. Offer counter-suggestions and probe for responses.
> Present related tasks and probe students' reasoning. Offer counter-suggestions to see if learned
> ideas transfer to new but related ideas.

TYPICAL RESPONSE: Briefly summarize the arguments against Piaget's theory of cognitive development.

> argument: Piaget underestimated children's cognitive ability. Researchers have found that children can complete some cognitive tasks that are beyond their stage of reasoning if the task and language are familiar. Piaget counter-argues that these children are "developmentally ready" and that is why they can accomplish the tasks.

argument:	Piaget's notion of egocentrism occurs to a lesser degree than he described. Researchers have found that children can consider another's point of view if it is practical and familiar in context.
argument:	Piaget's notion of stages is not as clear as he thought. Some children can be in a higher stage for familiar tasks and a lower stage for less familiar tasks.
argument:	Piaget did not consider culture and its influences on cognitive development.

TYPICAL RESPONSE: How do neo-Piagetian and constructivists views differ?

neo-Piagetian:	Neo-Piagetians attempt to account for the fact that cognitive development proceeds at different rates on different tasks by looking at problems that share the same logical structures or require the same number of logical steps.
constructivist:	Constructivists view cognitive development as a process in which children actively build systems of meaning and understandings of reality through their experiences and interactions.

2. KEY CONCEPTS, PRINCIPLES, AND THEORIES

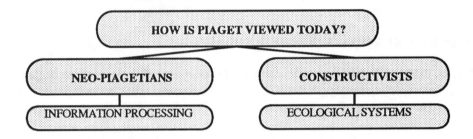

IV. HOW DID VYGOTSKY VIEW COGNITIVE DEVELOPMENT?

1. SELF-CHECK ITEM: On your comparison chart, enter information comparing and contrasting the views of Piaget and Vygotsky on the nature of learning and the context in which learning takes place. Describe in detail an example of a teaching strategy that applies Vygotskian concepts in the classroom.

TYPICAL RESPONSE: On your chart, compare and contrast the views of Piaget and Vygotsky.

	PIAGET	VYGOTSKY
NATURE OF LEARNING	learning occurs as an individual seeks equilibration	learning occurs when children are within their zone of proximal development
CONTEXT	assimilation and accommodation	turn shared knowledge into personal knowledge

TYPICAL RESPONSE: Describe a teaching strategy that applies Vygotskian principles in the classroom.

strategy:	Provide children with support during the early stages of learning; then, diminish support and have them take on increasing responsibility as they are able (scaffolding).
strategy:	Test both levels of the zone of proximal development to determine children's current states (dynamic assessment).

2. KEY CONCEPTS, PRINCIPLES, AND THEORIES

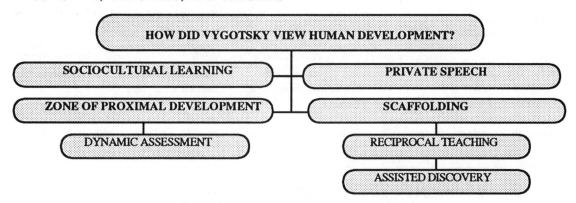

V. HOW DID ERIKSON VIEW PERSONAL AND SOCIAL DEVELOPMENT?

1. SELF-CHECK ITEM: Compare Erikson's eight stages of psychosocial development to Piaget's four stages of cognitive development on your comparison chart. Which of Erikson's stages pertain to preschool, elementary school, middle school, and high school students? Think of an example in which an individual experiences and successfully resolves each psychosocial crisis that occurs before and during the school years. In each instance, give an example of how a parent or teacher might help a child to resolve the development crisis in a positive way.

TYPICAL RESPONSE: Compare Piaget with Erikson and show how each pertains to students.

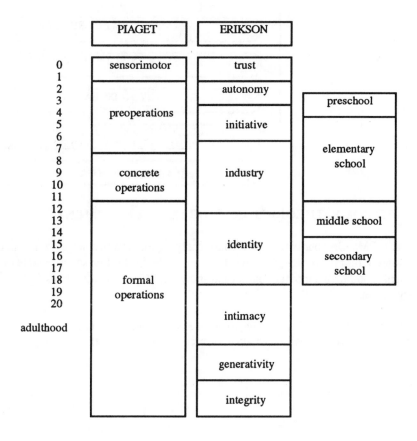

TYPICAL RESPONSE: Give an example of how a parent or teacher might help a child to successfully resolve tasks.

STAGES	EXAMPLE	POSITIVE RESOLUTION
initiative vs. guilt	learning language	whole language approach where children explore structure and meaning of words
industry vs. inferiority	learning to relate to others outside the family	provide opportunities for children to interact with peers
identity vs. role confusion	answer question "Who am I?"	provide adolescents with opportunities to "try on" roles

2. KEY CONCEPTS, PRINCIPLES, AND THEORIES

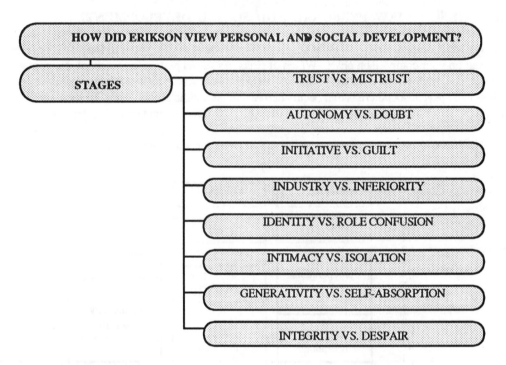

HOW DID ERIKSON VIEW PERSONAL AND SOCIAL DEVELOPMENT?

STAGES

TRUST VS. MISTRUST

AUTONOMY VS. DOUBT

INITIATIVE VS. GUILT

INDUSTRY VS. INFERIORITY

IDENTITY VS. ROLE CONFUSION

INTIMACY VS. ISOLATION

GENERATIVITY VS. SELF-ABSORPTION

INTEGRITY VS. DESPAIR

VI.   WHAT ARE SOME THEORIES OF MORAL DEVELOPMENT?

1. SELF-CHECK ITEM: On your comparison chart, compare Piaget's two stages of moral development to Kohlberg's six stages of moral reasoning. By what school levels do children seem capable of each level of thinking? Think of an original example of a moral dilemma and show how different individuals' judgments would illustrate each of Kohlberg's levels.

TYPICAL RESPONSE: Compare Piaget's two stages of moral development to Kohlberg's six stages on your comparison chart. By what school levels do children seem capable of each level of thinking?

PIAGET	KOHLBERG

	PIAGET	KOHLBERG
elementary	heteronomous morality (under six) autonomous morality (over six)	level one: preconventional (under 10)
secondary		level two: conventional (10-20) level three: postconventional (over 20)

TYPICAL RESPONSE: Think of an original example of a moral dilemma and show how different individuals' judgments would illustrate each of Kohlberg's levels. In each case, how might a parent or teacher help a child to grow?

example: Jake is an average math student and so are his two friends, Margaret and Bill. Before an upcoming weekly exam, Margaret and Bill steal a test copy from the teacher's desk. They ask Jake if he would like to look at the copy, but he declines. Jake decides to tell the teacher about Margaret and Bill stealing the test.

Level One: Jake tells the teacher because he is afraid of being implicated in the theft. He does not want to be punished. He may even be rewarded by the teacher for his act of honesty.

Level Two: Jake wants to please his teacher. Also, rules are rules -- no cheating.

Level Three: Jake, being a person of principle, could not disregard the agreement of the class to not cheat or his own belief that cheating is ethically wrong.

Kohlberg believed that children progress from one stage to the next by interacting with others whose reasoning is one or two stages above their own. Parents and teachers then need to identify the stage at which an individual is reasoning, then present examples of higher levels of reasoning about the same issue for him or her to consider.

2. KEY CONCEPTS, PRINCIPLES, AND THEORIES

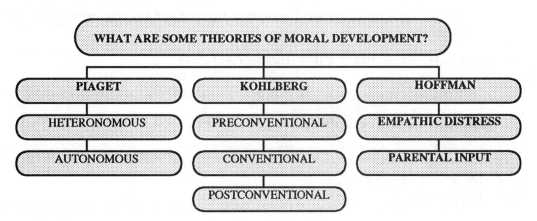

FOR YOUR ENJOYMENT

This section of the study guide includes suggestions for enriching your understanding of a chapter heading you have mastered. You will find information on activities related to the headings and suggestions for research papers, interviews, or presentations.

I. WHAT ARE SOME VIEWS OF HUMAN DEVELOPMENT?

1. Discuss the following controversies about development.
   A. Is development continuous or discontinuous?
   B. Is development universal or do culture, gender, or socioeconomic status play a role?

2. For a research topic, review the literature on cognitive, psychosocial, or moral development. What trends have emerged since Piaget, Erikson, or Kohlberg developed their theories?

II. HOW DID PIAGET VIEW DEVELOPMENT?

1. Ask children the following questions, then discuss the implications of the responses you receive.
   A. Where does the sun come from in the morning? Where does the sun go at night?
   B. Where do dreams come from? Where do they go when you wake up?
   C. When is yesterday? When is tomorrow?

2. Design a lesson plan for concrete operational children or formal operational adolescents that addresses the important cognitive tasks of the stage.

3. Critique a teacher's manual. Does it address important Piagetian concepts? Are the lesson suggestions developmentally appropriate?

4. For a research topic, review the literature on Piaget and his contributions to education.

III. HOW IS PIAGET VIEWED TODAY?

1. Ask children of different ages (e.g., ages 4, 7, and 11) to solve conservation problems as posed by Piaget. Adapt the problems so that their context and language are familiar to the child. Are there differences in the how the child solves unfamiliar and familiar tasks?

2. For a research topic, review the literature on neo-Piagetian and constructivists views of cognitive development.

IV. HOW DID VYGOTSKY VIEW DEVELOPMENT?

1. For a research topic, review the related literature on Vygotsky and his contributions to education.

V. HOW DID ERIKSON VIEW DEVELOPMENT?

1. Design a lesson that addresses the psychosocial needs of students who are at the age you intend to teach.

2. For a research topic, review the related literature on Erikson and his contributions to education.

VI. WHAT ARE SOME THEORIES OF MORAL DEVELOPMENT?

1. Interview five people using Kohlberg's "Heinz" dilemma. Categorize the responses.

2. For a research topic, review the related literature on Kohlberg and his contributions to education.

3. For a research topic, review the related literature on gender differences in moral reasoning.

CHAPTER TWO: SELF-ASSESSMENT

DIRECTIONS: Below are questions related to the main ideas presented in the chapter. Correct answers or typical responses can be found at the end of the study guide.

1.   According to Piaget, most elementary school children between the ages of 7 and 11, whose thinking is decentered and reversible, are in which stages of cognitive development?

   A. formal operations
   B. concrete operations
   C. preoperations
   D. sensorimotor

2.   Teaching strategies based on Vygotsky's work suggest that when children are capable of learning tasks they have reached, but have not yet begun to learn, teachers should assist learning through any of the following methods EXCEPT

   A. social interaction and private speech.
   B. assisted discovery and problem solving.
   C. conservation tasks.
   D. scaffolding.

3.   The psychosocial crisis associated with the high school years is

   A. identity vs. role confusion.
   B. industry vs. inferiority.
   C. intimacy vs. isolation.
   D. integrity vs. despair.

4.   Which of the following situations best illustrates the process of assimilation?

   A. A student adopts a new approach to a writing assignment after realizing that an approach learned earlier won't work.
   B. A child learns that she can be noisy when Grandma visits, but must be quiet and polite around Aunt Charlotte.
   C. A student learns how to crack the security code for the school's computer.
   D. A child attempts to ice skate by moving his legs in the same way that he does when he roller skates.

5.   Piaget's principles have been criticized on the basis of findings showing that

   A. many individuals go through the stages in a different order.
   B. cognitive tasks such as conservation cannot be taught unless the child is in the appropriate stages.
   C. the clarity of task instructions can significantly influence young children's performance on conservation tasks.
   D. children, on the average, are actually less competent that Piaget thought and rarely reach the different stages at the designated levels.

6.   Match the following stages of cognitive development with its brief description.

        _____ sensorimotor   A. Learning occurs largely through trial and error.

        _____ preoperations   B. Mental symbols can be used to represent objects.

        _____ concrete operations   C. Reversible mental operations are developed.

        _____ formal operations   D. Abstract thinking is possible; problems can be solved
                                            systematically.

7.   Match the following stages of Kohlberg's theory to descriptions of each.

        _____ preconventional   A. Do what the rule says, regardless of the consequences.

        _____ conventional   B. If I get caught, I was bad.

        _____ postconventional   C. Before judging her, let's consider her situation and motives.

8.   Refer to the scenario at the beginning of the chapter. Change the grade level in each of these cases, and discuss how the teaching techniques, as well as potential student reactions, will vary. For example, what if Mr. Jones had a college student or Ms. Lewis had twelfth graders or Ms. Quintera had first graders?

9.   Using Vygotsky's principle of zone of proximal development, describe the difference between a child's independent reading level and his or her instructional reading level.

10.   Describe Hoffman's theory of moral behavior and parenting. What is empathic distress?

PRACTICE TEST ANSWERS

1. False; Developmental characteristics need to be considered when making effective teacher decisions.

2. True; Development refers to the relatively permanent changes that occur over a lifespan.

3. False; Children are not miniature adults. Their thinking is quantitatively and qualitatively different from adult thinking.

4. C, B, A; Piaget studied cognition, Erikson studied personal growth and social relationships, and Kohlberg studied moral development (as did Piaget; however, Kohlberg is considered the major theorist).

5. Continuous theories address development as a smooth progression from infancy to adulthood. An example of continuous developmental theories would be information processing and ecological systems.

6. Discontinuous theories address development as a series of stages with major tasks to be accomplished at each stage. Piaget, Erikson, and Kohlberg are all discontinuous developmental theorists.

7. Schemes; Schemes are mental patterns or building blocks used to organize thinking.

8. Assimilation; Assimilation is the process of incorporating new objects or events into existing schemes.

9. Accommodation; Accommodation is the process of changing an existing scheme so that new objects or events can be understood.

10. C, D, A, B; Inferred reality occurs at the concrete operational stage, hypothetical thought is a product of formal operations, object permanence is a sensorimotor stage task, and egocentric behavior occurs during preoperations, according to Piaget.

11. A; Conservation is the ability to understand that even though a variable changes in appearance (as when water is poured from a short, wide beaker into a tall, narrow one), other characteristics (volume) remain constant.

12. D; Hypothesis testing is a characteristic of formal operations.

13. B; The abilities that make up formal operational thought -- thinking abstractly, testing hypotheses, and forming concepts that are independent of physical reality -- are critical in the learning of higher order thinking skills.

14. True; Piaget held the belief that development precedes learning, that developmental stages are largely fixed, and that certain cognitive tasks require readiness.

15. False; Piaget has been criticized for not considering the impact of culture and context on developmental stages.

16. False; Researchers have found that children can consider another's point of view if the context is practical and familiar.

17. C; Developmentally appropriate education attends to environments, curricula, materials, and teaching methodologies that are suitable for students in terms of their cognitive abilities and needs.

18. B; Constructivists view cognitive development as a process in which children actively build systems of meaning of reality through interactions with the environment.

19. A; Bronfenbrenner's ecological systems theory views development within a complex system of relationships.

20. Implications of Piaget's theory include: 1) focusing on process, not just product; 2) actively involving children in their own learning; 3) de-emphasizing educational practices that make children adult-like in their thinking; and 4) accepting individual differences.

21. True; Vygotsky emphasized the sociocultural nature of learning.

22. False; Vygotsky believed mental functioning exists within conversation and collaboration before it exists within the individual.

23. Zone of Proximal Development; The term refers to a phase of learning in which the child will fail alone, but succeed with assistance.

24. Private Speech; A mechanism emphasized by Vygotsky for turning shared speech into personal knowledge is private speech.

25. Scaffolding; Scaffolding means providing a child with support during the early stages of learning and then diminishing that support.

26. Dynamic Assessment; Vygotsky advocates testing both levels of the zone of proximal development. This approach is used when teachers give hints and prompts at different levels of complexity.

27. One implication of Vygotsky's theory is to expose children to other's effective problem solving strategies that fall within their zones. An example of this is cooperative learning. A second implication is to incorporate scaffolding into lessons. Reciprocal teaching and assisted discovery are examples that use scaffolding.

28. True; Erikson proposed that individuals pass through eight states with tasks at each stage.

29. True; When crises are not resolved, they reoccur later.

30. False; Erikson believed the opposite -- that the environment played a major role in causing and resolving developmental crises.

31. C, B, A, D; Attending to the question "Who am I?" develops identity. Focusing on "I am what I learn." develops industry. Exploring the physical and social environment develops initiative. And, finding oneself in another develops intimacy.

32. Initiative can be developed through exploration of the environment. Industry can be developed by allowing children to try things independently. Identity can be developed by supporting adolescents as they "try on" different adult roles.

33. Heteronomous Morality; This is a type of moral reasoning in which rules are fixed and made by others.

34. Autonomous Morality; This type of moral reasoning incorporates intentions and circumstances into the decision.

35. Moral Dilemma; Kohlberg's structured moral situations are called dilemmas.

36. A, C, B; At the preconventional level, individuals obey rules to avoid punishment. At the conventional level, individuals follow social rules. At the postconventional level, individuals use self-determined ethical principles to guide behavior.

37. A; According to Kohlberg, individuals move to higher levels of moral reasoning as they are exposed to them through others.

38. B; Hoffman's theory of moral development compliments Piaget and Kohlberg because it recognizes the role of cognitive abilities and reasoning skills in explaining moral behavior.

39. Limitations of Kohlberg's theory include: 1) Kohlberg's research was conducted using males, then generalized to females. 2) Kohlberg's theory deals with moral reasoning rather than moral behavior.

3
DEVELOPMENT DURING CHILDHOOD AND ADOLESCENCE

CHAPTER OVERVIEW

The purpose of this chapter is to expand upon the information presented in the previous chapter by addressing changes in physical, cognitive, and socioemotional development during the early childhood, elementary, middle, and high school years. Each period of development is described briefly below.

Development during the early childhood years involves the strengthening of large and small motor movements, the acquisition of language, the transition from sensorimotor to preoperational thought, and the formation of initiative.

Development during the elementary years involves tremendous physical growth, the transition from preoperational to concrete operational thought, a movement away from parent and family relations and toward peers, and the formation of industry.

Development during the middle and high school years involves puberty, the transition from concrete operational to formal operational thought, a dependence on peer relationships, and the formation of identity.

CHAPTER OUTLINE

I. HOW DO CHILDREN DEVELOP DURING THE PRESCHOOL YEARS?
    A. Physical Development in Early Childhood
    B. Language Acquisition
    C. Bilingual Education
    D. Socioemotional Development

II. WHAT KINDS OF EARLY CHILDHOOD EDUCATION EXIST?
    A. Day Care Programs
    B. Nursery Schools
    C. Compensatory Preschool Programs
    D. Early Intervention
    E. Kindergarten Programs
    F. Developmentally Appropriate Practice

III. HOW DO CHILDREN DEVELOP DURING THE ELEMENTARY YEARS?
    A. Physical Development During Middle Childhood
    B. Cognitive Abilities
    C. Socioemotional Development in Middle Childhood
    D. Parenting Styles and Moral Behavior

IV. HOW DO CHILDREN DEVELOP DURING THE MIDDLE AND HIGH SCHOOL YEARS?
    A. Physical Development During Adolescence
    B. Cognitive Development
    C. Characteristics of Hypothetical-Deductive Reasoning
    D. Implications for Educational Practice

E. Socioemotional Development During Adolescence
F. Identity Development
G. Erikson's Four Identity Statuses
H. Self-Concept and Self-Esteem
I. Social Relationships
J. Emotional Development
K. Problems of Adolescence

PRACTICE TEST

DIRECTIONS: Each chapter heading from the text listed below is followed by a series of related questions worth a total of ten points. Respond to each question, check your answers with those found at the end of the chapter, then determine your score. Consider nine points per heading to be mastery.

For those headings on which you do not score at least nine points, turn to the FOR YOUR INFORMATION section of the study guide for corrective instruction. For those headings on which you do score at least nine points, turn to the FOR YOUR ENJOYMENT section of the study guide for enrichment activities.

I. HOW DO CHILDREN DEVELOP DURING THE PRESCHOOL YEARS?

True or False

1. (1point) _____ A major physical accomplishment for children during the preschool years is an increase in control over large (gross) muscle activity and, to a lesser extent, over small (fine) muscle activity.

2. (1 point) _____ During the preschool years, children develop verbal (spoken) language, independent reading skills, and the fundamentals of writing.

Sentence Completion

3. (1 point) _____ A term used to describe preschool children's understanding of print -- that letters represent sounds, that spaces between words have meaning, and that books have a front and a back -- is ___.

4. (1 point) _____ The term used to describe a range of teaching practices that emphasizes students reading entire stories, articles, and other real materials rather than concentrating on isolated reading skills is ___.

Multiple Choice

5. (1 point) _____ According to Erikson, preschool children are attempting to resolve which of the following socioemotional issues?

A. initiative vs. guilt
B. trust vs. mistrust
C. identity vs. role confusion
D. intimacy vs. isolation

6. (1 point) _____ Which of the following parenting styles is identified as the most effective in helping children to be independent, self-assertive, friendly, and cooperative?

   A. authoritarian
   B. permissive
   C. authoritative
   D. passive

7. (1 point) _____ All of the following are types of collaborative efforts that promote healthy partnerships between parents and schools EXCEPT

   A. involvement in decision making, governance, and advocacy.
   B. teachers who provide at-home services.
   C. involvement with community organizations.
   D. parent volunteers who assist teachers in the classroom.

Short Answer/Essay

8. (3 points) Briefly describe how friendships, prosocial behaviors, and play contribute to healthy socioemotional development.

_____

_____

II. WHAT KINDS OF EARLY CHILDHOOD EDUCATION PROGRAMS EXIST?

True or False

9. (1 point) _____ Almost all countries of the world recognize that the beginning of formal school occurs when children are about six years old.

10. (1 point) _____ There is widespread agreement regarding schooling practices for children who are under six years of age.

Matching

11. (5 points) _____ programs that exist primarily to provide child-care services for working parents

   _____ planned programs where children learn "readiness" skills that prepare them for formal instruction

   _____ programs such as Head Start for children from disadvantaged backgrounds

   _____ programs that facilitate development for infants (from six months) and young children from disadvantaged backgrounds

   _____ programs just prior to first grade that prepare students for formal instruction by encouraging social skill development

   A. compensatory preschool programs

   B. day care programs

   C. early intervention programs

   D. kindergarten

   E. nursery school programs

Short Answer/Essay

12. (3 points) List three characteristics associated with developmentally appropriate educational practices.

_____

_____

_____

III. HOW DO CHILDREN DEVELOP DURING THE ELEMENTARY YEARS?

True or False

13. (1 point) _____ During the elementary years, physical development speeds up in comparison with earlier childhood.

14. (1 point) _____ "Transescents" are those individuals who are moving from early to middle childhood.

15. (1 point) _____ Between the ages of five and seven, children make the transition from preoperational to concrete operational thought.

Multiple Choice

16. (1 point) _____ An important area of personal and social development for elementary children is

A. identity.
B. generativity.
C. self-concept.
D. morality.

17. (1 point) _____ Which of the following statements can be attributed to preadolescent development?

A. Major growth spurts for preadolescents begin at about fourth grade for boys and at about sixth grade for girls.
B. While preadolescents feel their parents love them, they do not think they are understood.
C. Preadolescents are beginning the transition from preoperational to concrete operational thought.
D. A major concern of preadolescents is the development of initiative.

Short Answer/Essay

18. (2 points) List two developmental facts suggested by Thornburg that parents and teachers need to remember when working with preadolescents.

_____

_____

19. (3 points)   List three emotional concerns related to the physical, cognitive, and social development of adolescents.

_____

_____

_____

IV. HOW DO CHILDREN DEVELOP DURING THE MIDDLE AND HIGH SCHOOL YEARS?

True or False

20. (1 point)   _____   Early adolescence is a time of rapid physical and intellectual development. Middle adolescence is a time of adjustment to these changes. Later adolescence is of time of transition from childhood to adulthood.

21. (1 point)   _____   Puberty is a series of physiological changes that renders the immature organism capable of reproduction.

22. (1 point)   _____   Researchers believe that those who enter puberty early have an easier time adjusting to the physiological changes than those who enter puberty later in adolescence.

Multiple Choice

23. (1 point)   _____   According to Piaget, adolescence is a time of transition from

A. identity vs. role confusion to intimacy vs. isolation.
B. preoperations to concrete operations.
C. initiative vs. guilt to identity vs. role confusion.
D. concrete operations to formal operations.

24. (1 point)   _____   All of the following class activities are designed to promote hypothetical-deductive thought EXCEPT

A. Have students write a paper that requires them to look at more than one side of an issue.
B. Have students memorize definitions to terms.
C. Have students participate in a mock debate.
D. Have students critique their own position papers on a controversial topic.

25. (1 point)   _____   Which of the following terms means "a tendency to think about what is going on in one's own mind"?

A. reflectivity
B. cognition
C. hypothetical thought
D. inductive thought

26. (1 point) _____ Which of the following is a term used by Erikson to describe "not having a sense of one's identity"?

    A. conformity
    B. identity diffusion
    C. autonomy
    D. identity foreclosure

Short Answer/Essay

27. (3 points) List three problems associated with adolescence.

_____

_____

_____

_____

SCORING	POINTS NEEDED FOR MASTERY	POINTS RECEIVED
I. HOW DO CHILDREN DEVELOP DURING THE PRESCHOOL YEARS?	9	_____
II. WHAT KINDS OF EARLY CHILDHOOD EDUCATION PROGRAMS EXIST?	9	_____
III. HOW DO CHILDREN DEVELOP DURING THE ELEMENTARY YEARS?	9	_____
IV. HOW DO CHILDREN DEVELOP DURING THE MIDDLE AND HIGH SCHOOL YEARS?	9	_____

FOR YOUR INFORMATION

    This section of the study guide includes suggestions for further study of a heading you have not yet mastered. You will find information on: 1) typical responses to the SELF-CHECK item(s) from the text; and 2) key concepts, principles, and theories addressed in the text chapter.

I. HOW DO CHILDREN DEVELOP DURING THE PRESCHOOL YEARS?

1. SELF-CHECK ITEM: Begin a three-column comparison chart with the columns headed Early Childhood, Middle Childhood, and Adolescence. Enter information concerning early childhood (from the list in the text). Work from memory first to record what you can and then review the section to make your entries more complete.

TYPICAL RESPONSE: Begin a comparison chart on early childhood.

	EARLY CHILDHOOD	MIDDLE CHILDHOOD	ADOLESCENCE
AGES	three to five		
GRADE LEVELS	preschool		
PIAGETIAN STAGES	from sensorimotor to preoperations		
ERIKSONIAN STAGES	initiative vs. guilt		
SOCIOEMOTIONAL DEVELOPMENT	egocentric; play experiences with peers; self-expression; conflict and cooperation		
SOCIAL RELATIONSHIPS	seek out those who are developmentally similar, based on equality		
PHYSICAL CHARACTERISTICS	become more coordinated; develop preference for one side of body; gain control of gross and fine muscles		
LANGUAGE AND THOUGHT	develop verbal, reading (emergent literacy), and writing skills		
COGNITIVE ABILITIES	tied to present experiences		
SOURCES OF IMPACT ON DEVELOPMENT	home and family		

2. KEY CONCEPTS, PRINCIPLES, AND THEORIES

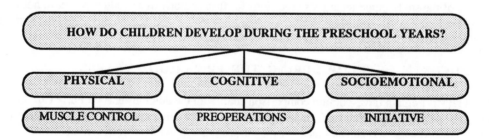

II. WHAT KINDS OF EARLY CHILDHOOD EDUCATION PROGRAMS EXIST?

1. SELF-CHECK ITEM: Distinguish the day care center, nursery school, compensatory preschool, and kindergarten as alternative approaches to early childhood education. What do research findings suggest about the value of early intervention, compensatory readiness training, and kindergarten retention? What is meant by developmentally appropriate practice?

TYPICAL RESPONSE: Distinguish between the day care center, nursery school, compensatory preschool, and kindergarten.

day care center:	Day care centers exist primarily to provide child-care services for working parents.
nursery school:	Like a day care center, nursery schools provide child-care services for working parents. However, a planned program that fosters social and cognitive development (readiness) is provided.
compensatory preschool:	These are programs, like Head Start, that are designed to increase school readiness for preschool children from disadvantaged backgrounds.
kindergarten:	Programs for preschoolers that take place one year prior to entry into the first grade. The purpose of kindergarten is to promote social skills.

TYPICAL RESPONSE: What do research findings suggest about the value of early intervention, compensatory readiness training, and kindergarten retention?

early intervention:	Several studies show that early intervention programs can have strong effects on students. These effects have lasted into the elementary grades.
compensatory readiness:	Research on Head Start programs has generally found positive effects related to children's readiness to enter the elementary grades.
kindergarten retention:	Research has shown that, while retention improves children's performance relative to their grademates in the short run, it is detrimental in the long run.

TYPICAL RESPONSE: What is meant by developmentally appropriate practice?

Developmentally appropriate practice is instruction based on students' characteristics and needs, not their ages. Different levels of ability, development, and learning styles are expected, accepted, and used to design curriculum. Developmentally appropriate practice has renewed earlier innovations in education such as non-graded primary and elementary schools, individualized instruction, and learning centers.

2. KEY CONCEPTS, PRINCIPLES, AND THEORIES

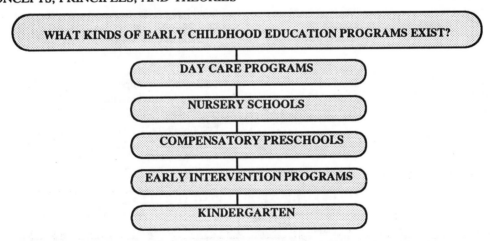

III. HOW DO CHILDREN DEVELOP DURING THE ELEMENTARY YEARS?

1. SELF-CHECK ITEM: Continue the comparison chart you began earlier, adding information in each category for middle childhood. Later, how will you be able to clearly distinguish features of early and middle childhood?

41

TYPICAL RESPONSE: Add information about middle childhood to your comparison chart. Distinguish between early and middle childhood.

	EARLY CHILDHOOD	MIDDLE CHILDHOOD	ADOLESCENCE
AGES	three to five	five to 12	
GRADE LEVELS	preschool	elementary	
PIAGETIAN STAGES	from sensorimotor to preoperations	from preoperations to concrete operations	
ERIKSONIAN STAGES	initiative vs. guilt	industry vs. inferiority	
SOCIOEMOTIONAL DEVELOPMENT	egocentric; play experiences with peers; self-expression; conflict and cooperation	independent action; cooperation with groups; performing in socially acceptable ways	
SOCIAL RELATIONSHIPS	seek out those who are developmentally similar, based on equality	peers become more important (early on, same-sex relationships)	
PHYSICAL CHARACTERISTICS	become more coordinated; develop preference for one side of the body; control of gross and fine muscles	physical development slows; period of adjustment to major changes during preschool years	
LANGUAGE AND THOUGHT	development of verbal, reading (emergent literature), and writing skills	language and thought become more complex	
COGNITIVE ABILITIES	tied to present experiences	rapidly developing memory and cognitive skills including ability to think about thinking	
SOURCES OF IMPACT ON DEVELOPMENT	home and family	family relationships become less important; peer relationships become more important	

2. KEY CONCEPTS, PRINCIPLES, AND THEORIES

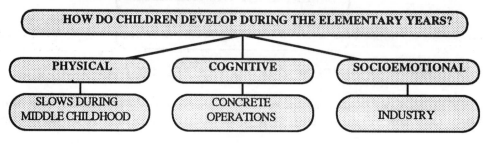

42

IV. HOW DO CHILDREN DEVELOP DURING THE MIDDLE AND HIGH SCHOOL YEARS?

1. SELF-CHECK ITEM: Add information about adolescence in the last column of your chart, using the same categories as before. Later, how will you be able to clearly distinguish features of middle childhood and adolescence? Re-read the scenario at the beginning of this chapter, and explain the interaction between Jake and Billy in terms of what you have learned about child development.

TYPICAL RESPONSE: Add information about middle and high school years to your comparison chart. Distinguish between middle childhood and adolescence.

	EARLY CHILDHOOD	MIDDLE CHILDHOOD	ADOLESCENCE
AGES	three to five	five to 12	12 to adulthood
GRADE LEVELS	preschool	elementary	middle and secondary
PIAGETIAN STAGES	from sensorimotor to preoperations	from preoperations to concrete operations	from concrete operations to formal operations
ERIKSONIAN STAGES	initiative vs. guilt	industry vs. inferiority	identity vs. role confusion
SOCIOEMOTIONAL DEVELOPMENT	egocentric; play experiences with peers; self-expression; conflict and cooperation	independent action; cooperation with groups; performing in socially acceptable ways; concern for fairness	appearance of reflectivity; define self; use of intellectual skills that permit consideration of possibilities
SOCIAL RELATIONSHIPS	seek out those who are developmentally similar, based on equality	peers become more important (early on, same-sex relationships)	peers are the focus; friendships, popularity, dating, and sexual relationships important
PHYSICAL CHARACTERISTICS	become more coordinated; develop preference for one side of the body; control of muscles	physical development slows; period of adjustment to major changes during the preschool years	onset of puberty; adult-like in appearance
LANGUAGE AND THOUGHT	development of verbal, reading, and writing skills	language and thought become more complex	language and thought become adult-like
COGNITIVE ABILITIES	tied to present experience	rapidly developing memory and cognitive skills including ability to think about thinking	hypothetical-deductive reasoning ability
SOURCES OF IMPACT ON DEVELOPMENT	home and family	family relationships become less important; peers become more important	peers; opposite-sex relationships form

TYPICAL RESPONSE: Explain the interaction between Billy and Jake (scenario at beginning of chapter).

Billy, a first grader, is beginning in the middle childhood stage of development. Physically, his development is slowing as he adjusts to the major growth spurt of early childhood. He is most likely making the transition from preoperations to concrete operations. In Erikson's terms, he is working on industry issues. He is becoming independent, learning how to cooperate with groups, and focusing on fairness when rules are concerned.

Jake, at 13, is entering adolescence. Physically, he is beginning puberty and is moving away from childhood to adulthood. He is most likely making the transition from concrete operations to formal operations. In Erikson's terms, he is working on identity issues. He is becoming reflective, using intellectual skills that permit him to think about possibilities, and comparing himself to others. Peers and opposite-sex relationships are the focus.

2. KEY CONCEPTS, PRINCIPLES, AND THEORIES

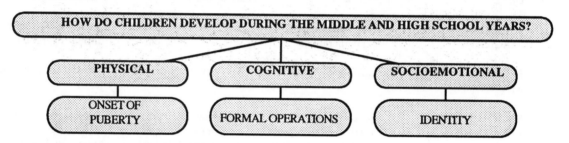

FOR YOUR ENJOYMENT

This section of the study guide includes suggestions for enriching your understanding of a chapter heading you have mastered. You will find information on activities related to the heading and suggestions for research papers, interviews, or presentations.

I. HOW DO CHILDREN DEVELOP DURING THE PRESCHOOL YEARS?

1. Interview or observe a preschool child. Make note of his or her physical, cognitive, and socioemotional development. Compare each with information from the text.

2. For a research topic, review the literature on development during the preschool years.

II. WHAT KINDS OF EARLY CHILDHOOD EDUCATION PROGRAMS EXIST?

1. Interview a day care worker, a nursery school teacher, or a Head Start teacher about the services they provide for children.

2. For a research topic, review the literature on early childhood education and developmentally appropriate practices.

III. HOW DO CHILDREN DEVELOP DURING THE ELEMENTARY YEARS?

1. Interview or observe an elementary school child. Make note of his or her physical, cognitive, and socioemotional development.

2. For a research topic, review the literature on elementary children's development.

IV. HOW DO CHILDREN DEVELOP DURING THE MIDDLE AND HIGH SCHOOL YEARS?

1. Interview or observe an adolescent. Make note of his or her physical, cognitive, and socioemotional development.

2. For a research topic, review the literature on topics related to adolescents.

CHAPTER THREE: SELF-ASSESSMENT

DIRECTIONS: Below are questions related to the main ideas presented in the chapter. Correct answers or typical responses can be found at the end of the study guide.

1. Which of the following cognitive abilities do children usually have when they enter first grade?

   A. understand abstract concepts
   B. understand an almost infinite variety of sentences
   C. use systematic approaches to solving problems
   D. concentrate for long periods of time

2. All of the following statements about play are true EXCEPT

   A. psychologists today generally agree that play is overemphasized in kindergarten and distracts from cognitive training.
   B. parallel play occurs when children do no interact purposefully with each other to create shared experiences.
   C. sociodramatic play developmentally follows pretend play.
   D. because play is spontaneous and nonreflective, it appears to stimulate creativity.

3. Participation in compensatory preschool programs has been found to

   A. benefit middle class children more than lower class children.
   B. increase disadvantaged children's readiness for kindergarten and first grade.
   C. have stronger effects on long term achievement than on initial achievement.
   D. be of little benefit to children under the age of two.

4. During the elementary years, children in middle childhood typically develop all of the following characteristics EXCEPT

   A. decentered thought.
   B. academic self-concept.
   C. preoperational thought.
   D. preadolescent peer group conformity.
   E. fear of not having a best friend.

5. During the middle school and high school years, most adolescents typically exhibit all of the following characteristics EXCEPT

   A. identity foreclosure.
   B. reflectivity.
   C. ability to reason hypothetically.
   D. growing demand for autonomy.
   E. variability in the onset of puberty.

6.   Match each developmental challenge below with the period of development in which it is most likely to occur.

_____ identity diffusion   A. early childhood

_____ friendship   B. middle childhood and preadolescence

_____ prosocial behavior   C. adolescence

_____ intimacy

_____ verbal language

_____ sociodramatic play

_____ conflict management

7.   According to Hoffman and Saltzstein, all of the following are approaches that parents use to discipline their children EXCEPT

A. love withdrawal.
B. retention.
C. power assertion.
D. induction.

8.   Refer to the scenario at the beginning of the chapter. Draw a web, map, or other visual picture of key influences on early elementary students such as Billy as well as one for middle school students such as Jake. Do students like Billy and Jake seek approval from the same sources? How does Jake affect Billy's self-concept? How does Billy affect Jake's self-concept?

9.   Develop an outline for an essay that would begin with the following thesis statement: Child development has important implications for classroom instruction at each grade level" Include an example for each grade level that would help to prove the thesis.

PRACTICE TEST ANSWERS

1. True; Physical development during the preschool years involves gaining control over muscle movements.

2. True; During the preschool years, children develop language, reading, and writing skills.

3. Emergent Literacy; Before they begin school, young children have often learned that letters represent sound, that spaces have meaning, and that books have a front and a back.

4. Whole Language; The term whole language is used to refer to a broad range of teaching practices that attempt to move away from the teaching of reading as a set of discrete skills.

5. A; Erikson's initiative vs. guilt stage of socioemotional development begins at about age three and continues until about age six.

6. C; Authoritative parents attempt to direct their children's behavior in ways that respect children's abilities, but at the same time express their own standards of behavior.

7. D; Providing at-home services is not suggested as a type of collaborative effort that promotes healthy partnerships between parents and schools.

8. Friendship contributes to healthy socioemotional development as children become aware of the thoughts and the feelings of others, which leads to give-and-take relationships. Prosocial behaviors are voluntary actions toward others such as caring, sharing, comforting, and cooperation -- all of which contribute to healthy socioemotional development. Play contributes to development because it promotes new skills and abilities.

9. True; In almost all the countries of the world, children begin their formal schooling at about six years of age.

10. False; There is widespread disagreement regarding schooling practices for children who are under six years of age.

11. B, E, A, C, D; Day care programs provide child care services. Nursery schools are like day care programs except they teach "readiness" skills. Compensatory preschool programs, such as Head Start, provide services to children who are disadvantaged. Early intervention programs provide services to infants and to young children who are disadvantaged. Kindergarten programs encourage skill development just prior to first grade.

12. Each child is viewed as a unique person with individual developmental needs. Curriculum and instruction are responsive to individual differences. Children are allowed to move at their own pace in acquiring academic skills. Extensive use is made of projects, play, exploration, group work, and learning centers.

13. False; During the elementary years, physical development slows so that the body can adjust to the changes that occurred during the preschool years.

14. True; Transecents are in transition from childhood to adolescence.

15. True; Between the ages of five and seven, children move from preoperations to concrete operations.

16. C; An important area of personal and social development for elementary school children is self-concept or self-esteem.

17. B; Preadolescents, still depending heavily on their parents, report that they are not understood.

18. Two developmental facts include: 1) preadolescents are breaking up their well-defined, predicable behavior and attitudes; and 2) preadolescents need guidance.

19. Emotional concerns of adolescents include not being accepted into a peer group, not having a best friend, being punished, having parents divorce, not doing well in school, and getting hurt.

20. True; Adolescence is a time of rapid physical and intellectual change, adjustments to the changes, and movement toward adulthood.

21. True; The purpose of puberty is to make individuals capable of reproduction.

22. False; The opposite is true -- researchers believe that those who enter puberty early have more difficulty adjusting than do those who enter puberty late.

23. D; According to Piaget, adolescents are moving from concrete operations to formal operations.

24. B; Having students memorize definitions does not necessarily promote hypothetical-deductive thought: the ability to consider possibilities.

25. A; Reflectivity is the tendency to think about one's own thinking.

26. B; Erikson calls the experience of not having a sense of one's identity "identity diffusion."

27. Problems associated with adolescence include emotional disorders, drug and alcohol abuse, delinquency and violence, risk of pregnancy, and risk of AIDS.

4
STUDENT DIVERSITY

CHAPTER OVERVIEW

In the previous two chapters, developmental similarities were discussed. The purpose of this chapter is to point out individual differences. Below are some of the ways in which students differ that can affect educational progress.

Diversity in culture can impact student learning.

Diversity in socioeconomic status can affect student learning.

Diversity in ethnicity and race can affect students' school experiences.

Diversity in language can affect student learning.

Diversity in gender can affect students' school experiences

Diversity in intelligence and learning styles can impact student achievement.

CHAPTER OUTLINE

I. WHAT IS THE IMPACT OF CULTURE ON STUDENT LEARNING?

II. HOW DOES SOCIOECONOMIC STATUS AFFECT STUDENT ACHIEVEMENT?
    A. The Role of Child Rearing Practices
    B. The Link Between Income and Achievement
    C. The Role of Schools as Middle Class Institutions
    D. Implications for Teachers

III. HOW DO ETHNICITY AND RACE AFFECT STUDENTS' SCHOOL EXPERIENCES?
    A. Racial and Ethnic Composition of the United States
    B. Academic Achievement of Minority Group Students
    C. Why Have Minority Group Students Lagged in Achievement?
    D. The Effect of School Desegregation

IV. HOW DO LANGUAGE DIFFERENCES AND BILINGUAL PROGRAMS AFFECT STUDENT ACHIEVEMENT?
    A. Bilingual Education
    B. Effectiveness of Bilingual Programs

V. HOW DO GENDER AND GENDER BIAS AFFECT STUDENTS' SCHOOL EXPERIENCES?
    A. Do Males and Females Think and Learn Differently?
    B. Sex-Role Stereotyping and Gender Bias

VI. HOW ARE STUDENTS DIFFERENT IN INTELLIGENCE AND LEARNING STYLES?
    A. Definitions of Intelligence
    B. Origins of Intelligence

C. Theories of Learning Styles
D. Aptitude Treatment Interactions

VII. WHAT IS MULTICULTURAL EDUCATION?
   A. Dimensions to Multicultural Education
   B. Assessing Effectiveness in Achieving Multicultural Goals

PRACTICE TEST

DIRECTIONS: Each chapter heading from the text listed below is followed by a series of related questions worth a total of ten points. Respond to each question, check your answers with those found at the end of the study guide chapter, then determine your score. Consider nine points per heading to be mastery.

For those headings on which you do not score at least nine points, turn to the FOR YOUR INFORMATION section of the study guide for corrective instruction. For those headings on which you do score at least nine points, turn to the FOR YOUR ENJOYMENT section of the study guide for enrichment activities.

I. WHAT IS THE IMPACT OF CULTURE ON STUDENT LEARNING?

True or False

1. (1 point) _____ There is probably as much cultural diversity within the United States as between the United States and other industrialized nations.

2. (1 point) _____ As a nation we tend to be tolerant of cultural differences within our borders.

Short Answer/Essay

3. (3 points) List three aspects of culture absorbed by children by the time they enter school.

_____

_____

_____

4. (5 points) List five ways in which students can differ.

_____

_____

_____

_____

_____

II. HOW DOES SOCIOECONOMIC STATUS AFFECT STUDENT ACHIEVEMENT?

True or False

5. (1 point) _____ Socioeconomic status (SES) refers to an individual's income, occupation, education, and prestige in society as well as race and ethnicity.

6. (1 point) _____ The home environment influences not only academic readiness but also the level of achievement throughout students' careers in school.

7. (1 point) _____ There is evidence that middle class teachers often have low expectations for lower class students and that the low expectations can cause low achievement.

Multiple Choice

8. (1 point) _____ All of the following child rearing practices for lower or middle socioeconomic status (SES) parents, on average, are true EXCEPT

A. lower SES parents want success for their children to a greater degree than do middle SES parents.
B. middle SES parents use high quality language when teaching their children.
C. middle SES parents reward their children to a greater degree for intellectual development than do lower SES parents.
D. middle SES parents encourage their children to read or participate in other learning activities.

9. (1 point) _____ Which of the following statements explains why students from backgrounds other than mainstream middle class might have difficulties in school?

A. Schools tend to place importance on individual rather than on group academic achievement.
B. Schools focus on future or on delayed rewards.
C. Most classrooms operate on the assumption that cooperation should be valued over competition.
D. Mainstream middle class students have learned to rely on families or on friends for academic support while other groups have not.

Short Answer/Essay

10. (5 points) Explain how student diversity in socioeconomic status can affect teachers.

_____

_____

_____

III. HOW DO ETHNICITY AND RACE AFFECT STUDENTS' SCHOOL ACHIEVEMENT?

Matching

11. (3 points) _____ primary groups of humans distinguished by form of hair, color of skin or eyes, and stature

A. ethnic group

B. minority group

_____ groups of humans distinguished by customs, characteristics, language, and common history

C. racial group

_____ group of people who is less in number and different from the dominate group in a nation, region, or community

51

Multiple Choice

12. (1 point) _____ According to the U.S. Census Bureau, which of the following statements about population trends is true?

A. The proportion of non-Hispanics is expected to decline in the next 20 years.
B. The proportion of Hispanics is expected to decline in the next 20 years.
C. The proportion of Asians is expected to decline by 14 percent by the year 2010.
D. The proportion of African Americans under 25 is expected to grow by 14 percent by the year 2010.

13. (1 point) _____ Prior to 1954, the policy of the U.S. educational system in many states was

A. to desegregate schools.
B. "separate but equal" education for African Americans.
C. to bus students in order to provide multicultural experiences for all students.
D. to create magnet schools in order to overcome segregation laws.

14. (1 point) _____ Which of the following Supreme Court decisions did away with legal school segregation?

A. Engle v. Vitale
B. Mills v. Board of Education of the District of Columbia
C. Nau v. Nichols
D. Brown v. Board of Education of Topeka

Short Answer/Essay

15. (4 points)   List four strategies that can be used to promote healthy diversity in schools.

_____

_____

_____

_____

IV. HOW DO LANGUAGE DIFFERENCES AND BILINGUAL PROGRAMS AFFECT STUDENT ACHIEVEMENT?

True or False

16. (1 point) _____ In the early 1980s, 13.3 percent of all U.S. children age five to 14 were from families in which the primary language spoken was not English.

17. (1 point) _____ Students whose dominant language is not English are more than twice as likely to be performing below grade level than are students from similar cultural backgrounds whose dominant language is English.

18. (1 point) _____ "English as a second language" programs are similar in nature and quality to "bilingual education" programs.

Sentence Completion

19. (1 point) _____ The term used to refer to those students who have not attained an adequate level of English proficiency to succeed in an English-only program is ___.

20. (1 point) _____ The term that is used to describe programs for students with limited proficiency in English which teach the students in their own language part time, while English is being used, is ___.

Short Answer/Essay

21. (2 points) List two arguments in favor of bilingual education.

_____

_____

Short Answer/Essay

22. (3 points) List three arguments against bilingual education.

_____

_____

_____

V. HOW DO GENDER AND GENDER BIAS AFFECT STUDENTS' SCHOOL EXPERIENCES?

True or False

23. (1 point) _____ All societies treat males differently than females; however, the roles occupied by each across cultures are broad.

24. (1 point) _____ Many of the observed differences between females and males can be linked to early socialization experiences.

Multiple Choice

25. (1 point) _____ All of the following statements regarding gender differences in learning are true EXCEPT

A. Studies generally find that males score higher than females on tests of general knowledge.
B. Females tend to score higher on tests of language.
C. There is no gender difference on tests of verbal ability.
D. Females tend to score higher on measures of abstract reasoning and memory.

Short Answer/Essay

26. (3 points) List three ways in which parents or adults reinforce sex role stereotyping and gender bias.

_____

_____

_____

27. (4 points)   List four ways in which teachers reinforce sex role stereotyping and gender bias.

_____

_____

_____

_____

VI. HOW ARE STUDENTS DIFFERENT IN INTELLIGENCE AND LEARNING STYLES?

Sentence Completion

28. (1 point) _____ The term used to describe a general aptitude for learning, including the ability to deal with abstractions and to solve problems, is ___.

29. (1 point) _____ The term used to represent a single score produced by Alfred Binet's test to represent the broad range of skills assessed by his test is ___.

30. (1 point) _____ Charles Spearman believed that there are variations in an individual's ability across tasks; however, he also believed in a general intelligence factor which he called ___.

Multiple Choice

31. (1 point) _____ Which of the following statements is true regarding intelligence and schooling?

A. Schooling has little or no effect on intelligence.
B. Intelligence is the primary factor that influences how well a student will perform in school.
C. IQ is not a fixed, unchangeable attribute, but rather is fluid and influenced by environmental factors.
D. What a student knows about a course beforehand (prior knowledge) is probably less important than intelligence.

32. (1 point) _____ Which of the following learning styles reflects the degree to which people perceive stimuli as whole patterns?

A. field dependence
B. field independence
C. impulsivity
D. reflectivity

33. (1 point) _____ Which of the following is a learning style representing the degree to which tasks are completed slowly with high emphasis on accuracy?

A. field dependence
B. field independence
C. impulsivity
D. reflectivity

Short Answer/Essay

34. (4 points) Explain how teachers can accommodate each type of learning style listed in the text.

_____

_____

_____

_____

VII. WHAT IS MULTICULTURAL EDUCATION?

True or False

35. (1 point) _____ Multicultural education encompasses all policies and practices schools might use to improve educational outcomes -- not only for students of different ethnic, social class, and religious backgrounds -- but also for students of different genders and exceptionalities.

36. (1 point) _____ The first step in multicultural education is for teachers and other school staff to learn about the cultures that make up their student body and to identify possible curriculum bias.

Short Answer/Essay

37. (4 points) List four ways in which a multicultural curriculum can be implemented in classrooms.

_____

_____

_____

38. (4 points) List four questions teachers can ask themselves about how they have made their classrooms culturally sensitive and gender fair.

_____

_____

SCORING	POINTS NEEDED FOR MASTERY	POINTS RECEIVED
I. WHAT IS CULTURAL DIVERSITY?	9	
II. HOW DOES SOCIOECONOMIC STATUS AFFECT STUDENT ACHIEVEMENT?	9	
III. HOW DO ETHNICITY AND RACE AFFECT STUDENTS' SCHOOL EXPERIENCES?	9	
IV. HOW DO LANGUAGE DIFFERENCES AND BILINGUAL PROGRAMS AFFECT STUDENT ACHIEVEMENT?	9	
V. HOW DO GENDER AND GENDER BIAS AFFECT STUDENTS' SCHOOL EXPERIENCES?	9	
VI. HOW ARE STUDENTS DIFFERENT IN INTELLIGENCE AND LEARNING STYLES?	9	
VII. WHAT IS MULTICULTURAL EDUCATION?	9	

FOR YOUR INFORMATION

This section of the study guide includes suggestions for further study of the information you have not yet mastered. You will find information on: 1) typical responses to the SELF-CHECK item(s) from the text; and 2) key concepts, principles, and theories addressed in the text chapter.

I.   WHAT IS THE IMPACT OF CULTURE ON STUDENT LEARNING?

1. SELF-CHECK ITEM: Define culture, list as many components of culture as you can think of, and then hypothesize about the impact of each one on student learning. Identify the elements in your own cultural identity and reflect on the impact of each element on your own school experience.

TYPICAL RESPONSE: Define culture, list its components, and hypothesize about the impact.

> Culture can be defined as the language, attitudes, ways of behaving, and other aspects of life (dress, values, interests, religion, food preferences, dance, hobbies, hair styles, etc.) that characterize a group of people. All of these aspects can influence student learning. While relatively homogeneous classrooms might be easier to teach (e.g. examples can be culturally relevant to all), the richness of diversity might be missed.

TYPICAL RESPONSE: Identify the elements in your own cultural identity and reflect on the impact of each element on your own school experience.

> This will include information on your racial, ethnic, and cultural background as well as your impression of how each has influenced your school experiences.

2. KEY CONCEPTS, PRINCIPLES, AND THEORIES

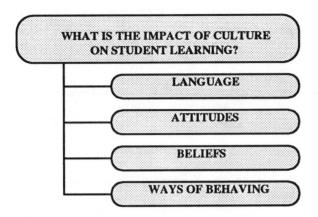

II. HOW DOES SOCIOECONOMIC STATUS AFFECT STUDENT LEARNING?

1. SELF-CHECK ITEM: Define socioeconomic status and explain how SES is (and is not) determined. Then identify three or more factors affecting school achievement that relate to social class background and give specific examples showing the impact of each factor.

TYPICAL RESPONSE: Define socioeconomic status and explain how SES is (and is not) determined.

> Socioeconomic status (SES) is a measure of prestige within a social group, usually based on income, education, and occupation. SES is usually based on a combination of an individual's income and years of education because these are most easily measured. SES is not determined by race or ethnicity.

TYPICAL RESPONSE: Identify three factors affecting school achievement relating to social class. Give examples.

child rearing practices:	quality of language used by parents with children activities parents expect of children (e.g., reading)
income:	lower class achievement affected by summer vacations
schools as middle class institutions:	future time orientation and focus on individuality

2. KEY CONCEPTS, PRINCIPLES, AND THEORIES

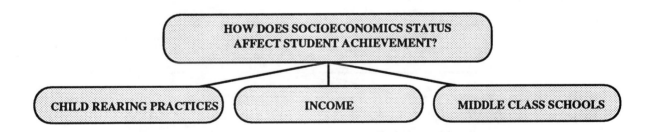

57

III. HOW DO ETHNICITY AND RACE AFFECT STUDENTS' SCHOOL EXPERIENCES?

1. SELF-CHECK ITEM: Define and distinguish among race, ethnic group, and minority group. In general, what are the differences in how well U.S. students of different races or ethnicities achieve? List as many cultural, social, economic, and historical factors as you can think of that help account for achievement differences. Assess the effectiveness of school desegregation and be prepared to argue its benefits or its failures.

TYPICAL RESPONSE: Define and distinguish between race, ethnic group, and minority group.

race:	groups of humans distinguished by form of hair, color of skin and eyes, and stature
ethnic group:	groups of humans distinguished by customs, characteristics, language, and common history
minority group:	group of humans who are less in number and different from the dominant group in a nation, region, or community

TYPICAL RESPONSE: In general, how well do American students achieve, by race or ethnicity, and what are the present trends?

In general, on virtually every test of academic achievement, African Americans, Mexican Americans, and American Indians score significantly lower than their Anglo-American cohorts. Often, they perform poorly because the instruction they receive is inconsistent with their cultural background and value system. Also, low expectations for minority group students can contribute to their low achievement. Current trends suggest that as minorities increasingly achieve economic security and enter the middle class, their children's achievement will come to resemble that of the dominant group.

TYPICAL RESPONSE: List as many cultural, social, economic, and historical factors that account for differences.

cultural	social	economic	historical
values	class	economic success	accurate cultural history
language	community status	academic preparation	
parenting styles	expectations	employment record	
family background	segregation	condition of school	

TYPICAL RESPONSE: Assess the effectiveness of school desegregation and argue its benefits or failures.

The overall effect of desegregation on the academic achievement of minority students has been small, though positive. When desegregation begins in elementary school and involves busing minority students to high quality schools, desegregation can have a significant effect on achievement. However, the schools to which minority students are bused are often no better than the segregated schools they leave behind.

2. KEY CONCEPTS, PRINCIPLES, AND THEORIES

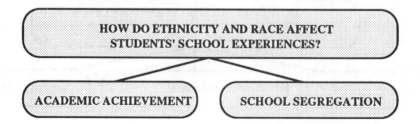

58

IV. HOW DO LANGUAGE DIFFERENCES AND BILINGUAL PROGRAMS AFFECT STUDENT ACHIEVEMENT?

1. SELF-CHECK ITEM: Define language minority and bilingual education and give examples of the many forms bilingual programs can take. According to research, which approaches to bilingual education are most effective? Which are the least?

TYPICAL RESPONSE: Define language minority and bilingual education and give examples of the many forms bilingual education can take.

language minority:	those individuals whose primary language spoken is not English
bilingual education:	refers to programs for students with limited proficiency in English that teach the students in their own language part of the time while English is being learned

TYPICAL RESPONSE: According to research, which approaches to bilingual education are most and least effective?

most effective:	Bilingual programs that emphasize culture and language as well as develop and maintain students' self-esteem and pride in both cultures are most effective.
least effective:	Programs that provide nothing more than minimum instruction in English as a second language are least effective.

2. KEY CONCEPTS, PRINCIPLES, AND THEORIES

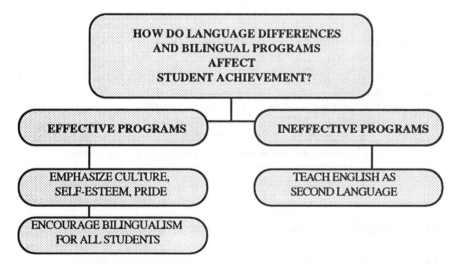

V. HOW DO GENDER AND GENDER BIAS AFFECT STUDENTS' SCHOOL EXPERIENCE?

1. SELF-CHECK ITEM: Use research findings and examples to support the view that cultural expectations and norms concerning gender are far more important than any actual differences as determinants of student achievement. Give three or more specific examples of gender bias commonly found in the classroom and state three or more general principles that teachers may apply for avoiding gender bias.

TYPICAL RESPONSE: Support the view that cultural expectations and norms concerning gender are more important than any real differences as determinants of student achievement.

Cross-cultural research indicates that the sex role is one of the first learned by individuals and that all societies treat males differently from females; therefore, sex role behavior is learned behavior. However, what is considered "natural" behavior for each gender is, in fact, based more on cultural beliefs than on biological necessity. Many of the observed differences between males and females can be clearly linked to differences in early socialization, according to research.

TYPICAL RESPONSE: Give three or more specific examples of gender bias found in the classroom.

Males engage in more interaction with their teachers in approval, instruction given, and being heard.
Teachers tend to punish females more promptly and explicitly for aggressive behavior.
Creative behavior of males is rewarded by teachers more often than is creative behavior of females.
Textbooks and curriculum promote gender bias (e.g., women's contributions to history are mostly ignored).
Teachers and other staff ignore instances of sexual harassment.
Teachers tend to choose males to boost their self-esteem and select literature with male protagonists.
The contributions of females are largely ignored on standardized tests.

TYPICAL RESPONSE: State three or more principles teachers may apply for avoiding gender bias.

Assign classroom jobs without regard to gender.
Avoid assigning males as group leaders and females as secretaries.
Refrain from using stereotypical behavior statements.
Avoid gender teams in competitive activities.
Encourage cross-gender collaboration.

2. KEY CONCEPTS, PRINCIPLES, AND THEORIES

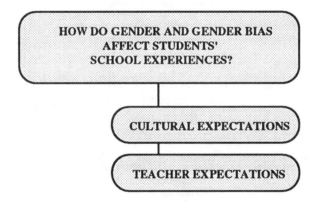

VI.   HOW ARE STUDENTS DIFFERENT IN INTELLIGENCE AND LEARNING STYLES?

1. SELF-CHECK ITEM: Define intelligence. Compare and contrast the general views of Binet, Spearman, Sternberg, Guilford, and Gardner about the nature of intelligence. Cite evidence supporting the claim that both heredity and environment play an important part in intelligence. Define learning styles and describe the traits that define field dependence, field independence, impulsivity, and reflectivity. List five or more characteristics of learning environments or conditions that individuals may prefer. Give specific examples of effective strategies teachers might use to accommodate learning styles and cultural based differences in classroom behaviors.

TYPICAL RESPONSE: Define intelligence. Compare and contrast the views of Binet, Spearman, Sternberg, Guilford, and Gardner about intelligence.

Intelligence can be defined as a general aptitude for learning or an ability to acquire and use knowledge or skills. Binet saw intelligence as a single score or intelligence quotient set at 100 for average (50th percentile). Spearman claimed that while there are variations in ability from task to task, there is a general intelligence factor (g) that exists across all learning situations. Sternberg described three types of intellectual ability:

60

intelligence, wisdom, and creativity. Guilford proposed 180 types of intelligences; six of mental operations times five of contents times six of products. Gardner described seven types intelligences: linguistic, musical, spatial, logical-mathematical, bodily, knowledge of self, and understanding of others.

TYPICAL RESPONSE: Cite evidence supporting the claim that both heredity and environment play an important role in intelligence.

> heredity: Children of high achieving parents are more likely to be high achieving themselves.

> environment: Schooling affects intelligence.

TYPICAL RESPONSE: Define learning styles and describe the traits that define field dependence, field independence impulsivity, and reflectivity.

> Learning styles can be defined as orientations or preferences for approaching learning tasks and processing information. Field dependent individuals tend to see patterns as a whole and tend to have difficulty separating out specific aspects of a situation or pattern. They are more oriented toward people and social relationships and tend to be better at history and literature. Field independent individuals see the parts that make up the large pattern. They prefer problems involving numbers and science. Impulsive individuals tend to work and to make decisions quickly. They finish work early and concentrate on speed. Reflective individuals take a long time to make decisions and to concentrate on accuracy.

TYPICAL RESPONSE: List five characteristics of learning environments or conditions that individuals may prefer.

> possible preferences affecting learning:
> perceptual information (visual, auditory, kinesthetic)
> amount of lighting (high, low)
> noise level (high, low)
> learning environment (competition, cooperation)
> temperature (hot, warm, cool, cold)

TYPICAL RESPONSE: Give examples of effective strategies teachers might use to accommodate learning styles and culture based on differences in classroom behaviors.

> Consider the amount of participation that each student might find excessive or limited.
> Watch for gesturing patterns which vary from culture to culture.
> Use humor and jokes in a way that is not intimidating or offensive.
> Consider touching patterns of cultures.
> Provide students with adequate personal space.

2. KEY CONCEPTS, PRINCIPLES, AND THEORIES

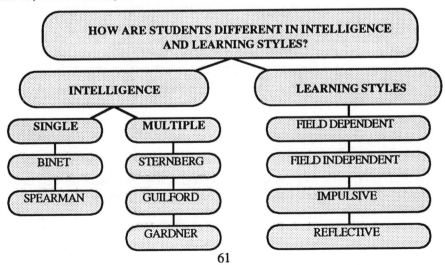

VII. WHAT IS MULTICULTURAL EDUCATION?

1. SELF-CHECK ITEM: Define multicultural education and describe its goals from both a narrow and broad perspective. Reread the case study at the beginning of this chapter. How, specifically should Marva and John proceed? How might multicultural education help them resolve the issues they have about the Thanksgiving pageant?

TYPICAL RESPONSE: Define multicultural education and describe its goals, both narrow and broad.

Multicultural education, in its simplest definition, emphasizes the inclusion of non-dominant group perspectives in the curriculum. Another definition lists multicultural education as all policies and practices schools might use to improve education outcomes, not only for students of different ethnic, social class, and religious backgrounds, but also for students of different genders and exceptionalities. A final definition of multicultural education is the idea that all students, regardless of groups to which they belong, should experience educational equality. The goals of multicultural education include reducing tracking, using a wide range of teaching methods, confronting racism and sexism, using bilingual education, and effectively mainstreaming students with exceptionalities.

TYPICAL RESPONSE: Reread the case at the beginning of this chapter. How, specifically, should Marva and John proceed? How might multicultural education help them resolve the issues they have about the Thanksgiving pageant?

Marva and John should make sure that the Thanksgiving pageant reflects the views of all those involved (perhaps looking at how cultures around the world offer thanks for bountiful harvests).

Marva and John should use resources that are free of stereotypes. Children of different racial or cultural backgrounds can play roles with which they are unfamiliar. For example, Navaho children can be pilgrims and girls can be hunters.

2. KEY CONCEPTS, PRINCIPLES, AND THEORIES

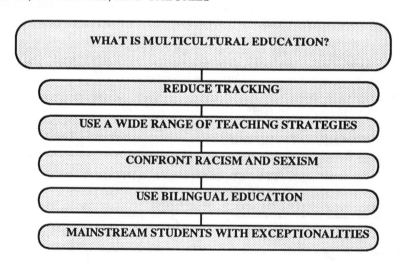

FOR YOUR ENJOYMENT

This section of the study guide includes suggestions for enriching your understanding of a chapter heading you have mastered. You will find information on activities related to the heading and suggestions for research papers, interviews, or presentations.

I. WHAT IS THE IMPACT OF CULTURE ON STUDENT LEARNING?

1. Design a bulletin board or other classroom display that addresses the beliefs, values, or traditions of a culture with which you are unfamiliar.

2. Create a lesson activity (e.g., role play) in which students must experience being a member of some minority group.

II. HOW DOES SOCIOECONOMIC STATUS AFFECT SCHOOL EXPERIENCES?

1. Interview several parents of difference socioeconomic backgrounds. What is their philosophy about education? about child rearing? about the condition of our nation's schools?

2. For a research paper, review the literature on the conditions of urban, suburban, and rural schools.

III. HOW DO ETHNICITY AND RACE AFFECT STUDENTS' SCHOOL EXPERIENCES?

1. For a research paper, review the literature on testing bias related to race.

IV. HOW DO LANGUAGE DIFFERENCES AND BILINGUAL PROGRAMS AFFECT STUDENT ACHIEVEMENT?

1. Debate the question: "Should English become our national language?" List several reasons why and why not.

2. For a research paper, review the literature on educational programs designed to address language differences.

V. HOW DO GENDER AND GENDER BIAS AFFECT STUDENTS' SCHOOL EXPERIENCES?

1. Observe a teacher for a few hours or a day. Are there differences related to gender in the ways students are approached, asked questions, disciplined, or rewarded?

2. For a research paper, review the literature on gender differences in schooling.

VI. HOW ARE STUDENTS DIFFERENT IN INTELLIGENCE AND LEARNING STYLES?

1. Create your own learning style profile using the following questions.
    A. What type of atmosphere is best for you when learning?
        1) quiet or some background noise (e.g., music)
        2) warm or cool room temperature
        3) bright or dark room
    B. What type of perceptual information do you prefer?
        1) visual
        2) auditory
        3) tactile, kinesthetic

VII. WHAT IS MULTICULTURAL EDUCATION?

1. For a research paper, review the related literature on multicultural education.

CHAPTER FOUR: SELF-ASSESSMENT

DIRECTIONS: Below are questions related to the main ideas presented in the chapter. Correct answers or typical responses can be found at the end of the study guide.

1. In a short essay, explain how multicultural education might have been implemented to address the goals of educational and social equality in your own school experience.

2. All of the following are defined as indicators of socioeconomic status EXCEPT

   A. occupation.
   B. race.
   C. income.
   D. education.

3. In teaching simple tasks to their children, low class mothers are more likely than middle class mothers to

   A. explain why the task needs to be done.
   B. give clear directions.
   C. take the child's perspective.
   D. demand that the task be done.

4. Multicultural education should be part of (a) the curriculum, (b) daily activities in the classroom and school, and (c) teachers' self-assessments. Give an example of each type of application.

5. The socioeconomic status of various racial and ethnic groups and the groups' scores on standardized tests appear to be

   A. positively correlated.
   B. negatively correlated.
   C. uncorrelated.

6. All of the following are disadvantages or limitations of bilingual programs EXCEPT

   A. Such programs generally interfere with performance in either the native language or English.
   B. The transition from a bilingual program to an English-only program may be difficult for many students.
   C. There are insufficient bilingual teachers to support such programs.
   D. The class groupings that result may conflict with the goals of desegregation.

7. Studies report all of the following findings EXCEPT

   A. Males score higher than females on tests of general knowledge.
   B. Females score higher than males on language measures.
   C. Females show more variability in performance than males.
   D. SAT math scores for females have been improving.

8. Through definitions and examples, distinguish among the concepts listed in (a) and (b) below.

   A. intelligence, intelligence quotient, multiple intelligence
   B. learning preferences, cognitive learning styles, cultural learning styles

9. Review the two points of view regarding teaching that are presented in the scenario at the beginning of the chapter. Write down how you would approach these cultural diversity issues in your classroom. How might gender, social class, religion, race, ethnicity, geographic region, ability and disability, and nationality be addressed in preparing for a Thanksgiving pageant? Are any classroom activities unaffected by these issues?

10. What are some specific ways in which cultural differences influence the ways students approach learning tasks?

11. In the following circumstances, should books or learning materials be eliminated from the school library shelves? Explain your answer.

    A. those using dialects that culturally or ethnically stereotype
    B. those using pictures of work or activities that stereotype by race or gender
    C. those found offensive by one ethnic or gender group

PRACTICE TEST ANSWERS

1. True; As much cultural diversity is likely to exist among groups as between groups.

2. False; As a nation, we tend to value characteristics of mainstream, high-status groups and devalue those of other groups.

3. By the time children enter school, they have absorbed many aspects of the culture in which they were raised: the language, beliefs, attitudes, ways of behaving, food preferences, and so on.

4. Socioeconomic status, Ethnicity, Race, Language, Gender, Intelligence, Learning style

5. False; Socioeconomic status refers to an individual's income, occupation, education, and prestige, but not his or her race or ethnicity.

6. True; The home environment can influence academic readiness and level of achievement.

7. True; There is evidence that teacher expectations influence achievement.

8. A; The degree to which lower SES parents want success for their children is not higher than middle SES parents.

9. A; Students from lower SES families are less willing to compete and are more interested in cooperation, sometimes viewed as cheating in middle class schools.

10. Teachers need to recognize that lower SES students might come from families where different (i.e., different from middle class schools) values are stressed, group needs take precedence over individual needs, the "here and now" is more important than the future, low income does not necessarily indicate low academic achievement, and parent-rearing styles differ from those of the mainstream.

11. C, A, B; A racial group can be defined as one of the primary groups of humans, distinguished by hair form, skin and eye color, and stature. An ethnic group is distinguished by common customs, language, and history. A minority group is a group of people who are less in number than the dominant group.

12. D; African Americans under 25 will grow by 14 percent by the year 2010.

13. B; separate but equal

14. D; Brown vs. the Board of Education of Topeka

15. Strategies for promoting healthy diversity include: be fair, provide equal opportunities for all, eliminate bias, encourage human interaction, use culture/gender fair texts and other curricular materials, assist students in valuing their heritage, avoid resegregation, provide support for language minority students, and use cooperative learning.

16. True; In the early 1980s, 13.3 percent of U.S. school-aged children did not speak English as a primary language.

17. True; When compared to students whose first language is English, students whose primary language is not not English are twice as likely to perform below grade level.

18. False; English as a second language programs are not as effective as bilingual programs, which teach students in their own language until they become proficient in English.

19. Limited English Proficient (LEP); refers to language minority student

20. Bilingual Education; Bilingual programs provide non-English instruction while English is being learned.

21. One reason is that lack of English proficiency is a major reason for academic failure for language minority students. A second reason is that learning a second language facilitates learning in one's own language.

22. One argument against bilingual education is the lack of teachers who are themselves bilingual. Another argument is that students have difficulty with the transition from the bilingual program to the all-English one. A final argument is that the goals of bilingual education sometimes conflict with those of desegregation because they remove students from classes containing English-speaking (often white) students.

23. True; Most societies treat females and males differently.

24. True; Many differences between males are females are learned.

25. D; Gender differences do not impact measures of abstract reasoning and memory.

26. From the moment they are born, males and females are viewed differently. After birth, males wear blue while females wear pink. Newborn babies are given sex-appropriate reinforcement and are handled differently. By school age, females are expected to be passive, nurturing, and dependent while males are expected to be more aggressive and independent.

27. Males receive more encouragement for creativity, engage in more interactions involving approval, instruction giving, and attention by teachers than do females. Females receive punishment more promptly and explicitly by teacher than males.

28. Intelligence; While there are several definitions, most theorists agree that intelligence involves an aptitude for learning.

29. IQ; Intelligence Quotient

30. g; which exists across all learning situations

31. C; Intelligence is not fixed, but rather is influenced by factors such as schooling.

32. A; Field dependent learners tend to see patterns as a whole.

33. D; Reflective learners are likely to spend a long time considering all alternatives.

34. Field dependent learners tend to be more oriented toward people and social relationships, better at recalling conversations and relationships, work best in groups, and prefer history and literature. Field independent learners do well with numbers, science, and problem solving tasks. Impulsive learners tend to work and make decisions quickly, while reflective types are more likely to consider all alternatives.

35. True; The definition of multicultural education goes beyond culture to encompass ethnic, class, religious, and gender differences.

36. True; Teachers and other school staff must understand diversity by learning about the cultures represented in their schools.

37. The curriculum should represent diverse perspectives, free of race, gender, and handicap stereotypes. It should provide information on contemporary and historical culture that includes more than the dominant view. It should draw on the experiences of the cultures represented by the students. It should allow equal access to all students.

38. Have I made efforts to respect the cultures of my students? Have I allowed students to speak freely? Has the curriculum reflected diversity? Have I avoided segregating students along cultural, gender, or other lines? Have I attempted to understand differences in values, beliefs, and perspectives of all my learners? Have I treated each student with respect?

5
BEHAVIORAL THEORIES OF LEARNING

CHAPTER OVERVIEW

To this point in the text, development -- how individuals change or adapt over time -- has been the focus. The purpose of this chapter, and the next few that follow, is to consider learning -- how individuals use developmental changes in order to understand their world. In particular, this chapter focuses on behavioral ideas about learning, some of which are listed below.

Behavioral theories of learning consider how individuals react to and interact with the environment.

Behavioral theories of learning evolved from Pavlov's classical conditioning to Thorndike's law of effect, to Skinner's operant conditioning.

Behavioral theories of learning (operant conditioning) involve principles and schedules of reinforcement.

Behavioral theories of learning include Bandura's observational learning where modeling and vicarious learning are considered.

Behavioral theories of learning can explain how academic achievement is affected by the environment.

CHAPTER OUTLINE

I. WHAT IS LEARNING?

II. WHAT BEHAVIORAL LEARNING THEORIES HAVE EVOLVED?
    A. I. Pavlov: Classical Conditioning
    B. E. L. Thorndike: The Law of Effect
    C. B. F. Skinner: Operant Conditioning

III. WHAT ARE SOME PRINCIPLES OF BEHAVIORAL LEARNING?
    A. The Role of Consequence
    B. Reinforcers
    C. Intrinsic and Extrinsic Reinforcers
    D. Punishers
    E. Immediacy of Consequences
    F. Shaping
    G. Extinction
    H. Schedules of Reinforcement
    I. Maintenance
    J. The Role of Antecedents

IV. HOW HAS SOCIAL LEARNING THEORY CONTRIBUTED TO OUR UNDERSTANDING OF HUMAN LEARNING?
    A. Bandura: Modeling and Observational Learning
    B. Meichenbaum's Model of Self-Regulated Learning

V. WHAT ARE SOME IMPLICATIONS OF BEHAVIORAL LEARNING APPROACHES FOR EDUCATION?
    A. Strengths and Limitations of Behavioral Learning Theories
    B. Behavioral, Social, and Cognitive Learning

PRACTICE TEST

    DIRECTIONS: Each chapter heading from the text listed below is followed by a series of related questions worth a total of ten points. Respond to each question, check your answers with those found at the end of the study guide chapter, then determine your score. Consider nine points per heading to be mastery.

    For those headings on which you do not score at least nine points, turn to the FOR YOUR INFORMATION section of the study guide for corrective instruction. For those headings on which you do score at least nine points, turn to the FOR YOUR ENJOYMENT section of the study guide for enrichment activities.

I. WHAT IS LEARNING?

True or False

1. (1 point)   _____   Learning is usually defined as a change in an individual caused by experience.

2. (1 point)   _____   Learning and development are separate and distinct phenomena.

3. (1 point)   _____   Learning occurs intentionally or unintentionally.

Multiple Choice

4. (1 point)   _____   Which of the following is a definition of learning from a behavioral perspective?

    A. Learning is the unobservable mental process that individuals use to learn and to remember information.
    B. Learning is taking in, processing, storing, and retrieving perceptual information.
    C. Learning is building new knowledge structures upon those previously learned.
    D. Learning includes how pleasurable or how painful consequences of behavior change individuals' behavior over time.

5. (1 point)   _____   Which of the following is an example of learning?

    A. An infant cries when he is frightened.
    B. A student wears her "lucky" shirt during a test.
    C. An adolescent becomes ill after being exposed to influenza.
    D. An athlete is fatigued after a vigorous workout.

Essay/Short Answer

6. (5 points)   List five things you learned as you read the chapter.

_____

_____

_____

_____

_____

II. WHAT BEHAVIORAL LEARNING THEORIES HAVE EVOLVED?

Matching

7. (3 points)   _____   the neutral stimulus becomes the conditioned stimulus which produces a conditioned response

                          _____   an unconditioned stimulus produces an unconditioned response while a neutral stimulus does not produce a response

                          _____   a neutral stimulus is paired with an unconditioned stimulus which produces an unconditioned response

A. preconditioning

B. conditioning

C. postconditioning

Multiple Choice

8. (1 point)   _____   Which of the following statements best depicts Thorndike's law of effect?

A. If an act is followed by a satisfying change in the environment, the chance that the act will be repeated increases.
B. If a previously neutral stimulus is paired with an unconditioned stimulus, the neutral stimulus becomes the conditioned stimulus.
C. Reflexive behaviors account for only a small proportion of all actions.
D. Less desired activities can be increased by linking them to more desired activities.

9. (1 point)   _____   Skinner used the term "operant" to refer to

A. behaviors as a response to the environment.
B. stimulus-response (S-R) theory.
C. the law of effect.
D. operating upon the environment in the absence of any known or unknown stimulus.

10. (1 point)   _____   Which of the following is an advantage of the Skinner box?

A. It showed that animal learning could be generalized to human learning.
B. It demonstrated the difference between rote and creative learning.
C. It allowed for careful scientific study of behavior in a controlled environment.
D. It showed that animals could learn from observing other animals.

Essay/Short Answer

11. (4 point)   Compare and contrast classical conditioning with operant conditioning.

_____

71

_____

_____

_____

III. WHAT ARE SOME PRINCIPLES OF BEHAVIORAL LEARNING?

Sentence Completion

12. (1 point) _____ Any consequences that strengthen behavior are called ___.

13. (1 point) _____ Reinforcers that satisfy basic human needs are called ___.

14. (1 point) _____ Reinforcers that acquire their value by being associated with reinforcers that satisfy basic human needs are called ___.

Matching

15. (5 points) _____ anything that increases a behavior by presenting something desired

                    _____ anything that decreases a behavior by removing something desired

                    _____ anything that decreases a behavior by adding something aversive

                    _____ eliminating or decreasing a behavior by removing its reinforcing agent

                    _____ anything that increases a behavior by preventing or removing something unpleasant from occurring

A. positive reinforcement

B. negative reinforcement

C. presentation punishment

D. removal punishment

E. extinction

Multiple Choice

16. (1 point) _____ Which of the following is an example of shaping?

    A. anything that is external to the activity, such as praise or good grades
    B. a signal as to what behavior(s) will be reinforced or punished
    C. the use of small steps combined with feedback to help learners reach goals
    D. the linking of less desired activities with more desired ones

17. (1 point) _____ A teacher gives short quizzes over lessons presented at random times during the unit. Which schedule of reinforcement is being depicted in the above scenario?

    A. fixed ratio (FR)
    B. variable ratio (VR)
    C. fixed interval (FI)
    D. variable interval (VI)

IV. HOW HAS SOCIAL LEARNING THEORY CONTRIBUTED TO OUR UNDERSTANDING OF HUMAN LEARNING?

Sentence Completion

18. (1 point) _____ The term used to describe the imitation of others' behavior is ___.

19. (1 point) _____ The term used to describe the process of learning from others' successes and failures is ___.

Essay/Short Answer

20. (4 points) List the phases of observational learning.

_____

_____

_____

_____

21. (4 points) List the steps involved in self-instruction (cognitive behavior modification) by using the terms cognitive modeling, self-regulation, and external guidance.

_____

_____

_____

_____

V. WHAT ARE SOME IMPLICATIONS OF BEHAVIORAL LEARNING FOR EDUCATION?

True or False

22. (1 point) _____ An advantage of behavioral learning theories is that they consider concept formation, problem solving, and thought processes.

23. (1 point) _____ An advantage to behavioral learning theories is that they explain much of human behavior and are useful in changing behavior.

24. (1 point) _____ Social learning theory, which is a direct outgrowth of behavioral learning theories, helps bridge the gap between behavioral and cognitive theories.

Short Answer/Essay

25. (4 points) List four applications of behavioral learning theories.

_____

_____

_____

26. (3 points)   List three instructional strategies that follow behavioral principles of learning.

_____

_____

_____

SCORING	POINTS NEEDED FOR MASTERY	POINTS RECEIVED
I. WHAT IS LEARNING?	9	
II. WHAT BEHAVIORAL LEARNING THEORIES HAVE EVOLVED?	9	
III. WHAT ARE SOME PRINCIPLES OF BEHAVIORAL LEARNING?	9	
IV. HOW HAS SOCIAL LEARNING THEORY CONTRIBUTED TO OUR UNDERSTANDING OF HUMAN LEARNING?	9	
V. WHAT ARE THE IMPLICATIONS OF BEHAVIORAL LEARNING APPROACHES FOR EDUCATION?	9	

FOR YOUR INFORMATION

This section of the study guide includes suggestions for further study of the information you have not yet mastered. You will find information on: 1) typical responses to the SELF-CHECK item(s) from the text; and 2) key concepts, principles, and theories addressed in the text chapter.

I. WHAT IS LEARNING?

1. SELF-CHECK ITEM: List examples of learning. As you read, identify your examples in terms of the kind of learning that takes place, and add new examples.

TYPICAL RESPONSE: List examples and types of learning.

TYPE OF LEARNING	EXAMPLE
classical conditioning	test anxiety, school phobia
operant conditioning	most types of school behaviors
observational learning	observing and modeling a teacher's behaviors

74

2. KEY CONCEPTS, PRINCIPLES, AND THEORIES

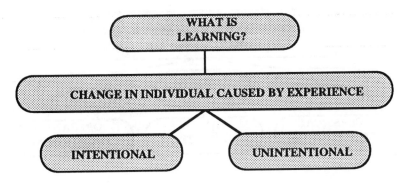

II. WHAT BEHAVIORAL LEARNING THEORIES HAVE EVOLVED?

1. SELF-CHECK ITEM: Develop a chart to compare and contrast the contributions of Pavlov, Thorndike, and Skinner to our understanding of learning. Chart headings might include, for example, name of theorist, name of theory, main concepts, and experiment (or research) conducted. Summarize the main research findings. What examples will you give of the applications of these findings to human learning?

TYPICAL RESPONSE: Develop a chart to compare learning theorists.

	THEORY	CONCEPTS	RESEARCH	APPLICATIONS
PAVLOV	classical conditioning	association of a neutral stimulus with an un-conditioned stimulus to produce a conditioned response	focused on observations and careful measurements	few educational applications; test anxiety, school phobia
THORNDIKE	law of effect	if an act is followed by a satisfying change in the environment, the chance that the act will be repeated in similar situations increases	worked with cats that learned how to escape from a box in order to get food	if learning produces satisfaction, more learning will occur
SKINNER	operant conditioning	consequences of one's behavior plays a crucial role in determining one's future behavior	Skinner box: allowed for careful scientific study of behavior in controlled environment	most learning experiences involve operant conditioning

2. KEY CONCEPTS, PRINCIPLES, AND THEORIES

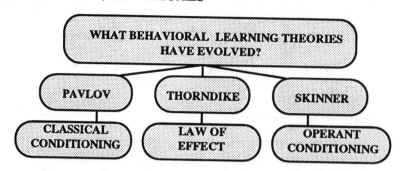

III. WHAT ARE SOME PRINCIPLES OF BEHAVIORAL LEARNING?

1. SELF-CHECK ITEM: Brainstorm a list of all the principles of behavioral learning you can remember, and think of a specific classroom example illustrating each one. Then, classify the items in your list in a concept map organized around the following headings: consequences, reinforcement, punishment, and antecedents.

TYPICAL RESPONSE: Brainstorm principles of behavioral theory and give examples.

TERM	DEFINITION	EXAMPLE
primary reinforcer	satisfies basic needs	food, water, security, warmth, sex
secondary reinforcer	a consequence that people learn to value through its relationship with a primary reinforcer	social reinforcers (praise, smiles, hugs, attention), activity reinforcers (toys, games, fun activities), token reinforcers (money, grades, stars, points)
positive reinforcer	presentation of desired consequence to strengthen a behavior	if they strengthen the behavior, praise, grades, attention
negative reinforcer	release from undesired consequence to strengthen a behavior	if they strengthen the behavior, a student is released from time out or other isolating situation
Premack principle	using favored activities to reinforce less favored ones	allowing students to go to the library once their work is completed
presentation punishment	presentation of undesired consequence to weaken a behavior	if they weaken the behavior, scolding, detention, name on board
removal punishment	removal of desired consequence to weaken a behavior	if they weaken the behavior, time out, loss of privilege
extinction	eliminating a behavior by removing reinforcement	if it eliminates the behavior, ignoring (i.e., neither reinforcing nor punishing the behavior)
shaping	reinforcing small steps with feedback	partial credit for work done that is nearly correct

cueing	information on which behaviors are to be reinforced or punished	telling students that an assignment will be worth ten points
discrimination	use of cues, signals, or information to know when behavior is likely to be reinforced or punished	praising students for correct responses and providing feedback for incorrect responses
generalization	perception of and response to similarities in stimuli	explaining to students that rules in the classroom also apply during lunch and recess

2. KEY CONCEPTS, PRINCIPLES, AND THEORIES

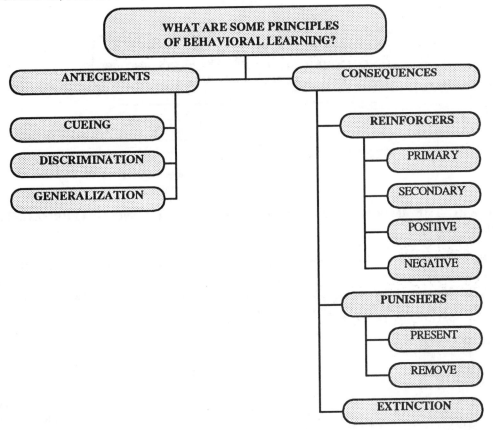

IV. HOW HAS SOCIAL LEARNING THEORY CONTRIBUTED TO OUR UNDERSTANDING OF HUMAN LEARNING?

1. SELF-CHECK ITEM: Extend the comparison chart you began earlier by adding the contributions of social learning theorists as represented by Bandura and Meichenbaum.

TYPICAL RESPONSE: Add social learning theorists to chart from.

	THEORY	CONCEPTS	RESEARCH	APPLICATIONS
BANDURA	social learning	focus is on effects of cues on behavior and on internal mental processes	observed how consequences of modeling influenced learning	**assure attention, model behavior, have students reproduce behaviors, evaluate, motivate**
MEICHENBAUM	cognitive behavior modification	focus is on self-instruction and self-regulation	worked on Vygotskian concepts (e.g., scaffolding)	**cognitive model, external guide, self guide**

2. KEY CONCEPTS, PRINCIPLES, AND THEORIES

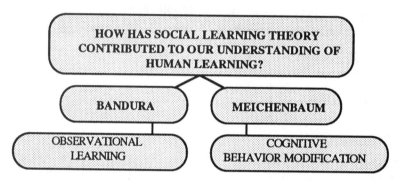

V. WHAT ARE THE IMPLICATIONS OF BEHAVIORAL LEARNING APPROACHES FOR EDUCATION?

1. SELF-CHECK ITEM: Use the concepts presented in this chapter to briefly explain what happened in Ms. Esteban's class in the scenario at the beginning of the chapter. Then, use the principles presented in this chapter to propose alternative solutions to the problem. Conclude by writing a one-sentence definition of learning that would encompass both the problem and solutions you proposed.

TYPICAL RESPONSE: Explain the problems in the scenario involving Ms. Esteban, then propose solutions.

PROBLEM	SOLUTION
Ms. Esteban wants her class to raise their hands, then wait to be called on before answering a question.	In order to increase their hand-raising and waiting behavior, Ms. Esteban needs to reinforce those specific behaviors (operant conditioning).
Ms. Esteban responds to a student who is not waiting to be called on before answering a question.	Ms. Esteban needs to ignore or punish (in the Skinnerian sense) those behaviors she does not want to occur (operant conditioning).
Elizabeth serves as a model for the other children when she does not wait to be called on -- as does Ms. Esteban when she responds to Elizabeth.	Since students learn by observing others, they need to see appropriate hand-raising behavior being modeled. Ms. Esteban should wait until she sees the type of behavior she wants and only then reinforce it (observational learning).

TYPICAL RESPONSE: Write a definition of learning.

Learning is related to the reinforcement of appropriate behaviors.

2. KEY CONCEPTS, PRINCIPLES, AND THEORIES

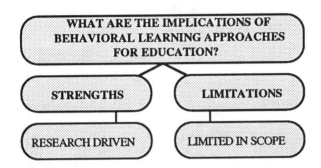

FOR YOUR ENJOYMENT

This section of the study guide includes suggestions for enriching your understanding of a chapter heading you have mastered. You will find information on activities related to the heading and suggestions for research papers, interviews, or presentations.

I. WHAT IS LEARNING?

1. Ask a variety of people to define learning. Analyze the responses to see which ones fit a behavioral definition of learning.

2. For a research paper, review the literature on the history of our understanding about learning through some of the writings of major behavioral (functionalism, associationism) theorists.

II. WHAT BEHAVIORAL LEARNING THEORIES HAVE EVOLVED?

1. For a research paper, review the literature on the history of behaviorism from introspection to physiological psychology to connectionism and to early behaviorism.

III. WHAT ARE SOME PRINCIPLES OF BEHAVIORAL LEARNING?

1. Observe in a classroom for one hour while video taping the events. Analyze the video tape by listing as many examples of behaviorism in action as you can. Look for some of the following behavioral principles: primary and secondary reinforcers, positive and negative reinforcers, Premack principle, shaping, chaining, extinction, schedules of reinforcement, cueing, discrimination, and generalization.

2. For a research paper, review the literature on the use of behavioral principles in everyday life.

IV. HOW HAS SOCIAL LEARNING THEORY CONTRIBUTED TO OUR UNDERSTANDING OF HUMAN LEARNING?

1. Observe in a classroom. List examples in which students observed a model, then imitated his or her actions.

2. For a research paper, review the literature on observational learning related to TV and to other media violence (for example). Include an explanation of the implications for educators.

V. WHAT ARE SOME IMPLICATIONS OF BEHAVIORAL APPROACHES FOR EDUCATION?

1. Design a management program for your future classroom. Include a list of class rules, motivators for following rules, and consequences for non-compliance.

2. Design a lesson using a behavioral approach (e.g., programmed instruction, mastery learning, outcome based education).

3. For a research paper, review the literature on behavioral approaches to schooling and learning.

CHAPTER FIVE: SELF-ASSESSMENT

DIRECTIONS: Below are questions related to the main ideas presented in the chapter. Correct answers or typical responses can be found at the end of the study guide.

1. Which of the following most clearly represents an example of learning?

    A. moving one's hand away from a hot object
    B. being startled by a loud noise
    C. feeling thirsty after exercising
    D. feeling anxious when a teacher announces a pop quiz

2. Match the following theories or laws of learning with a related experiment (a situation may be used more than once or not at all).

    _____ classical conditioning   A. Animals learned to press a lever to get food.

    _____ the Law of Effect   B. The behavior of children was observed after they had seen films in which adults acted aggressively.

    _____ operant conditioning

         C. Before reading a passage about Buddhism, students reviewed concepts of Christianity.

    _____ social learning theory

         D. Animals used trial and error to learn to escape from a box.

         E. Animals exhibited conditioned responses when they heard a tone.

3. An example of a primary reinforcer is

    A. safety or security.
    B. good grades in school.
    C. money.
    D. praise.
    E. access to toys.

4. What is the Premack Principle? Give two examples of classroom practices that clearly illustrate the Premack Principle.

5. Match these types of consequences with the most probable example of each.

_____ positive reinforcement   A. "Write 'I will not talk' 500 times."

_____ negative reinforcement   B. "Students who finish this work will not be assigned extra homework tonight."

_____ punishment   C. "Good job, class! I'm proud of you."

6. Attention, retention, reproduction, and motivation are four phases in

A. observational learning.
B. shading.
C. self-regulation.
D. reinforcement.

7. Meichenbaum's model for cognitive behavior modification involves all of the following concepts EXCEPT

A. self-regulated learning.
B. private speech.
C. vicarious learning.
D. modeling.

8. Refer to the scenario at the beginning of the chapter. Identify one or two behavioral principles that are evident in the scenario with Ms. Estaban.

9. Does punishment -- for example, reprimands or lost privileges -- work well with children? What are some negative effects of punishment? If punishment is ineffective and also produces negative side effects, why do so many teachers rely on it so much?

10. If teacher B.F. Skinner had lunch with teacher Albert Bandura to plan a strategy to correct the acting out behavior of a student of theirs, how would each describe his plan for modifying the student's behavior?

PRACTICE TEST ANSWERS

1. True; Learning is a change in behavior caused by experience rather than by innate abilities.

2. False; Learning and development are inseparably linked.

3. True; Sometimes learning is intentional and sometimes it is unintentional.

4. D; From a behavioral perspective, learning focuses on the consequences of behavior change.

5. B; The student "learns" (perhaps from having a positive experience the last time the shirt was worn) that the shirt is lucky.

6. Some things that could be learned include: the definition of learning, that learning can be intentional or unintentional, that Pavlov and Thorndike linked learning to reflexes, that your surroundings are incorporated into what you read, that a lot is known about learning, that the information is useful, etc.

7. C, A, B; During the preconditioning phase, an unconditioned stimulus produces an unconditioned response while a neutral stimulus does not produce a response (UCS produces an UCR); during the conditioning phase, a neutral stimulus is paired with an unconditioned stimulus which produces an unconditioned response (NS + UCS produces an UCR); and, during the postconditioning phase, the neutral stimulus becomes the conditioned stimulus which produces a conditioned response (CS produces a CR).

8. A; Thorndike's Law of Effect states that if an act is followed by a satisfying state of affairs, it is likely to be repeated.

9. D; Skinner means "operating" upon the environment.

10. C; According to your text, the Skinner box allowed for careful scientific study of behavior in a controlled environment.

11. Classical conditioning shows how learning can affect what was once thought to be involuntary, reflexive behavior. Operant conditioning shows how learning occurs in the absence of any unconditioned stimulus.

12. Reinforcers; increase the frequency of behavior

13. Primary Reinforcers; satisfy basic needs such as food, water, warmth, and sex

14. Secondary Reinforcers; satisfy needs that are associated with primary reinforcers such as money, grades, and praise

15. A, D, C, B, E; Reinforcers increase behavior. Positive reinforcers do so by presenting something desired following a targeted behavior. Negative reinforcers do so by removing something undesired following a targeted behavior. Punishers decrease behavior. Presentation punishers do so by presenting something undesired following a targeted behavior. Removal punishers do so by removing something desired following a targeted behavior. Extinction, where a behavior stops, occurs when behavior is neither reinforced nor punished.

16. C; A is an example of extrinsic rewards, B is cueing, and D is the Premack principle.

17. D; Variable interval reinforcement is available at some times, but not at others.

18. Modeling; the imitation of others' behavior

19. Vicarious Learning; learning from the experiences of others' successes or failures

20. Attentional Phase, Retention Phase, Reproduction, and Motivational Phase

21. Cognitive model in which instructor performs task using self-talk; External guidance in which student performs task with help from instruction; Self-guidance in which student performs task using self-talk; and, Self-instruction in which student uses faded self-guidance and private speech

22. False; Concept formation, problem solving, and thinking fall more into the domain of cognitive learning than behavioral learning.

23. True; Explaining and changing behaviors are central to behavioral learning theories.

24. True; Social learning theory helps bridge the gap between different learning perspectives.

25. Classroom management, behavioral objectives, task analysis, motivation, modeling, feedback, and reinforcement are all examples of behavioral theory applications.

26. Programmed instruction, mastery learning, and the Keller plan are instructional strategies based on behavioral principles.

6
COGNITIVE THEORIES OF LEARNING:
BASIC CONCEPTS

CHAPTER OVERVIEW

In the preceding chapter you were asked to consider learning as behavior. The purpose of this chapter is to consider learning as cognition -- how individuals take in, process, store, and retrieve environmental information. Some main ideas about cognition and learning are listed below.

Cognitive theories of learning use an information processing model that describe the functions of the sensory register, short term memory, and long term memory and explain how each contributes to the processing of information.

Cognitive theories of learning explain the processes of remembering and forgetting.

Cognitive theories of learning demonstrate how to improve memory by using paired-associate learning and serial and free recall learning.

Cognitive theories of learning explain how rote learning and meaningful learning differ.

Cognitive theories of learning describe metacognitive skills used to enhance learning.

Cognitive theories of learning identify effective study strategies that help students learn.

Cognitive theories of learning promote specific teaching strategies that help students learn.

CHAPTER OUTLINE

I. WHAT IS AN INFORMATION PROCESSING MODEL?
    A. Sensory Register
    B. Short Term or Working Memory
    C. What Factors Enhance Long Term Memory
    D. Levels of Processing
    E. Other Information Processing Models

II. WHAT CAUSES PEOPLE TO REMEMBER OR FORGET?
    A. Forgetting and Remembering
    B. Practice

III. HOW CAN MEMORY STRATEGIES BE TAUGHT?
    A. Verbal Learning
    B. Paired-Associated Learning
    C. Serial and Free Recall Learning

IV. WHAT MAKES LEARNING MEANINGFUL?
    A. Rote versus Meaningful Learning
    B. Schema Theory

V. HOW DO METACOGNITIVE SKILLS HELP STUDENTS LEARN?

VI. WHAT STUDY STRATEGIES HELP STUDENTS LEARN?
   A. Note Taking
   B. The PQ4R Method

VII. HOW DO COGNITIVE TEACHING STRATEGIES HELP STUDENTS LEARN?
   A. Making Learning Relevant and Activating Prior Knowledge
   B. Organizing Information

PRACTICE TEST

DIRECTIONS: Each chapter heading from the text listed below is followed by a series of related questions worth a total of ten points. Respond to each question, check your answers with those found at the end of the study guide chapter, then determine your score. Consider nine points per hearing to be mastery.

For those headings on which you do not score at least nine points, turn to the FOR YOUR INFORMATION section of the study guide for corrective instruction. For those headings on which you do score at least nine points, turn to the FOR YOUR ENJOYMENT section of the study guide for enrichment activities.

I. WHAT IS AN INFORMATION PROCESSING MODEL?

True or False

1. (1 point) _____ Perception of stimuli is more complex than reception of stimuli.

2. (1 point) _____ According to Gestalt psychologists, we tend to perceive whole units of information rather than the pieces of sensation and that the whole of the sensation equals more than the individual parts.

3. (1 point) _____ According to Gestalt psychologists, we attempt to separate figure -- that which we focus on -- from ground -- background.

Sentence Completion

4. (1 point) _____ The term used to refer to a storage system that can hold a limited amount of information for a few seconds is ___.

5. (1 point) _____ The term used to refer to a storage system that can hold an unlimited amount of information for long periods of time is ___.

Matching

6. (3 points) _____ type of memory that contains images of experiences organized by when and where they happened

             _____ type of memory that is organized in networks of connected ideas or relationships (schemas)

             _____ type of memory that is non-verbal and automatic in its aid to recall things we do well (e.g., bike riding or reading)

A. semantic memory

B. episodic memory

C. procedural memory

Short Answer/Essay

7. (1 point) Define "levels-of-processing."

_____

8. (1 point) Define "dual code" theory.

_____

II. WHAT CAUSES PEOPLE TO REMEMBER OR FORGET?

True or False

9. (1 point) _____ Most forgetting occurs because information in the sensory register was not transferred to long term memory.

10. (1 point) _____ Interference happens when to-be-measured information gets pushed aside by other information.

Matching

11. (4 points) _____ example: learning to drive on the right side of the road when first taught to drive on the left

A. retroactive inhibition

B. proactive inhibition

_____ example: when knowing a first language helps to learn a second

C. proactive facilitation

D. retroactive facilitation

_____ example: when learning a second language increases awareness of one's native language

_____ example: having no trouble recognizing the letter *b* until the letter *d* is introduced

Sentence Completion

12. (1 point) _____ When people attempt to learn lists, they tend to remember the first things and the last things presented. These effects are called ___.

Short Answer/Essay

13. (3 points) Give an example of each of the following methods of practice: distributed practice, part learning, and enactment.

_____

_____

_____

III. HOW CAN MEMORY STRATEGIES BE TAUGHT?

True or False

14. (1 point) _____ Students often learn things as facts before they understand them as concepts or skills.

15. (3 points)   List three examples of paired-associate learning.

_____

_____

_____

16. (3 points)   List three examples of serial learning.

_____

_____

_____

17. (3 points)   List three examples of free-recall learning.

_____

_____

_____

IV. WHAT MAKES INFORMATION MEANINGFUL?

Multiple Choice

18. (1 point) _____ Which of the following statements is true regarding meaningful learning?

A. We have limited ability to recall meaningful information; however, we can retain role information far more easily.
B. Mnemonic strategies are necessary for recall of meaningful information.
C. Meaningful learning refers to the memorization of facts or associations.
D. Meaningful learning is not arbitrary and it relates to information or concepts learners already possess.

19. (1 point) _____ Learned information that can be applied only to a restricted, often artificial, set of circumstances is called

A. rote knowledge.
B. declarative knowledge.
C. inert knowledge.
D. procedural knowledge.

20. (1 point) _____ Which of the following explains how knowledge is stored in memory?

A. It is thought to be stored in hierarchies.
B. Information enters and is stored in a random fashion.
C. It is thought to be stored as an outline.
D. Information that is most important is stored first and less important information follows.

Short Answer/Essay

21. (2 points)   Give two example of rote learning.

_____

_____

22. (2 points)   Give two examples of meaningful learning.

_____

_____

23. (3 points)   Explain the requirements necessary for meaningful learning to occur.

_____

_____

V. HOW DO METACOGNITIVE SKILLS HELP STUDENTS LEARN?

Sentence Completion

24. (1 point)   _____   The term used to refer to thinking about one's own thinking is ___.

Multiple Choice

25. (1 point)   _____   Which of the following is an example of a metacognitive skill?

    A. recalling a name
    B. listening to a lecture
    C. planning an effective study strategy
    D. reading a poem aloud

26. (1 point)   _____   Which of the following statements about metacognition is accurate?

    A. While most students do gradually develop adequate metacognitive skills, others do not.
    B. Although students develop metacognitive skills at different times, all eventually learn them.
    C. Looking for common elements in a given task is an ineffective study strategy.
    D. Self-talk hinders learning.

Short Answer/Essay

27. (7 points)   Make a list of metacognitive skills used by students in a variety of subjects.

_____

_____

_____

_____

VI. WHAT STUDY STRATEGIES HELP STUDENTS LEARN?

True or False

28. (1 point) _____ Research of the effectiveness of note taking has been inconsistent.

29. (1 point) _____ Summarization involves writing lengthy statements about all of the ideas presented in a text.

Sentence Completion

30. (1 point) _____ A study strategy in which main points of the material are presented in a hierarchical format, with each detail organized under a higher-level category is ___.

31. (1 point) _____ A study strategy in which main ideas are connected using a network-type diagram is ___.

Short Answer/Essay

32. (6 points) List the six steps of the PQ4R method.

_____

_____

_____

VII. HOW DO COGNITIVE TEACHING STRATEGIES HELP STUDENTS LEARN?

Matching

33. (5 points) _____ strategy using examples that are, in one respect, similar, but otherwise, unlike

A. advance organizer

B. analogy

_____ strategy linking prior knowledge to new information by thinking about it in a new way

C. conceptual model

_____ strategy using a diagram to show how concepts are related to each other

D. elaboration

E. questioning

_____ strategy in which the learning process is halted in order to assess learning

_____ strategy presenting a framework to the content prior to the learning experience

Short Answer/Essay

34. (3 points) Give three examples of strategies that enhance understanding and retention by activating prior knowledge.

_____

_____

_____

35. (2 points)   List two appropriate ways in which analogies can be used effectively.

_____

_____

SCORING	POINTS NEEDED FOR MASTERY	POINTS RECEIVED
I. WHAT IS AN INFORMATION PROCESSING MODEL?	9	_____
II. WHAT CAUSES PEOPLE TO REMEMBER OR FORGET?	9	_____
III. HOW CAN MEMORY STRATEGIES BE TAUGHT?	9	_____
IV. WHAT MAKES INFORMATION MEANINGFUL?	9	_____
V. HOW DO METACOGNITIVE SKILLS HELP STUDENTS LEARN?	9	_____
VII. WHAT STUDY STRATEGIES HELP STUDENTS LEARN?	9	_____
VII. HOW DO COGNITIVE TEACHING STRATEGIES HELP STUDENTS LEARN?	9	_____

FOR YOUR INFORMATION

This section of the study guide includes suggestions for further study of the information you have not yet mastered. You will find information on: 1) typical responses to the SELF-CHECK item(s) from the text; and 2) key concepts, principles, and theories addressed in the text chapter.

I.   WHAT IS AN INFORMATION PROCESSING MODEL?

1. SELF-CHECK ITEM: On the basis of your own understanding, draw a diagram representing the Atkinson-Shiffrin information processing model and label its parts. Using one specific example throughout, briefly explain how information is processed through each of the model's parts. How will you contrast the information processing model with other process models of learning and memory described in this section?

TYPICAL RESPONSE: Draw an information processing model.

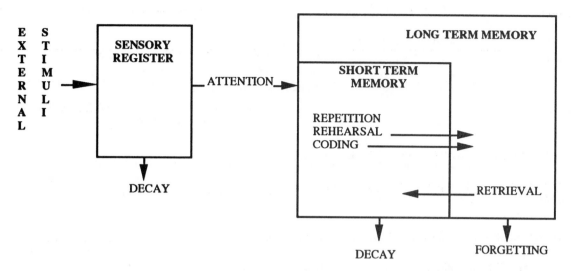

TYPICAL RESPONSE: Using one specific example throughout, briefly explain how information is processed.

Example: learning a new phone number

environmental stimuli	reading the number in the phone book (visual environmental stimuli)
sensory store	If the phone number is attended to, it will enter the memory system while other phone numbers on the page decay through inattention.
short term memory	If the phone number is to be remembered for a brief period of time, repetition of the number -- saying it over and over again -- will keep it available. Once the number is dialed, it decays.
long term memory	If the phone number is to be remembered so that it can be retrieved at a later time, then further processing is necessary (e.g., rehearsal, elaboration, or organization of the information). Forgetting is the inability to search and find stored information.

2. KEY CONCEPTS, PRINCIPLES, AND THEORIES

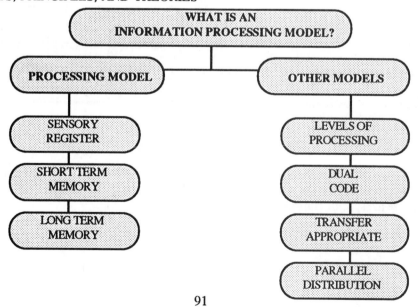

II. WHAT CAUSES PEOPLE TO REMEMBER OR FORGET?

1. SELF-CHECK ITEM: Read the scenario at the beginning of this chapter on Ms. Bishop's memory experiment. Using concepts from this section, offer two or more possible explanations for the instances of forgetting described in the case. Now suggest two or more possible explanations for the instances of remembering. How might the different kinds of "practice" enhance the students' learning in this case?

TYPICAL RESPONSE: In the scenario, why did students forget? Why did they remember? What strategies can enhance learning?

> One possible explanation for forgetting is that the students did not transfer information about the diagram from short term memory to long term memory so that it could be retrieved during the discussion. Another possible explanation for forgetting is that the amount of information being asked to remember exceeded short term memory capacity.

> One possible solution for remembering is that if students had a similar learning experience, they perhaps used it to facilitate their new learning experience. Another explanation is that some information was more salient than other information. For example, colors might be remembered more easily than text.

> Practice strategies that enhance memory include distributed practice, part learning, overlearning, and enactment.

2. KEY PRINCIPLES, CONCEPTS, AND THEORIES

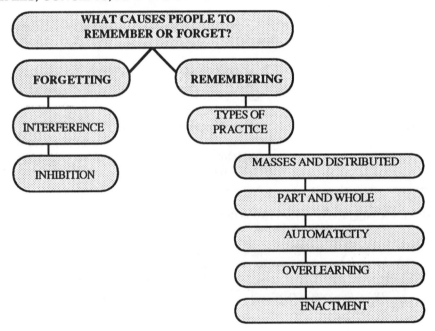

III. HOW CAN STRATEGIES BE TAUGHT?

1. SELF-CHECK ITEM: Sketch a concept map or diagram with MEMORY STRATEGIES at the center and spokes or arrows to three subgroups: PAIRED-ASSOCIATE, SERIAL, and FREE-RECALL. Then, try to correctly categorize the specific strategies described in this section.

TYPICAL RESPONSE: Sketch a concept map.

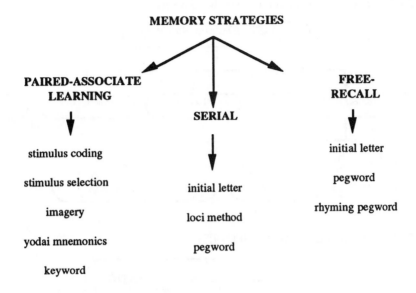

MEMORY STRATEGIES

PAIRED-ASSOCIATE LEARNING

stimulus coding

stimulus selection

imagery

yodai mnemonics

keyword

SERIAL

initial letter

loci method

pegword

FREE-RECALL

initial letter

pegword

rhyming pegword

2. KEY CONCEPTS, PRINCIPLES, AND THEORIES

See 2: SELF-CHECK ITEM above.

VI. WHAT MAKES INFORMATION MEANINGFUL?

1. SELF-CHECK ITEM: Explain the difference between rote and meaningful learning, the role of schemas in learning, and the importance of prior knowledge in learning. Contrast rote learning and meaningful learning by giving three examples of each one. Then, develop a model of a schema for one of your examples of meaningful learning. What aspects of your schema highlight the importance of background knowledge in learning?

TYPICAL RESPONSE: Explain rote and meaningful learning, the role of schemas in learning, and the importance of prior knowledge in learning.

Rote and meaningful learning differ in that rote learning refers to the memorization of facts or associations while meaningful learning refers to the non-arbitrary relationship between new information and prior knowledge. The role of schemas in learning is that as we learn new information or add to existing knowledge, we categorize elaborate, and organize it in a way we find meaningful. Prior knowledge facilitates new learning by meshing the two to bring a deeper understanding to each.

TYPICAL RESPONSE: Give three examples of rote and meaningful learning.

ROTE LEARNING	MEANINGFUL LEARNING
memorizing that 2/4 = 1/2	understanding that eating 2/4 of a cake is the same as eating 1/2 of a cake
memorizing the bones and muscles of the body	understanding that the muscular system and the skeletal system work together to create movement
memorizing the steps necessary for performing cardiopulmonary resuscitation (CPR)	understanding when cardiopulmonary resuscitation (CPR) is necessary and when it is not

93

TYPICAL RESPONSE: Develop a model for one of the above schemas.

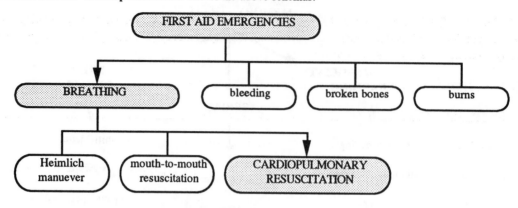

2. KEY CONCEPTS, PRINCIPLES, AND THEORIES

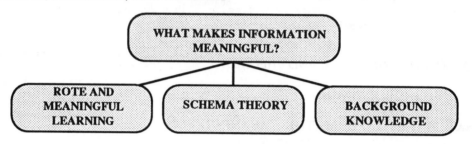

IV. HOW DO METACOGNITIVE SKILLS HELP STUDENTS LEARN?

1. SELF-CHECK ITEM: Define metacognition, then explain how self questioning is an example of the effective use of a metacognitive ability to promote learning.

TYPICAL RESPONSE: Define metacognition and explain how self-questions promote learning.

Metacognition means knowledge about one's own learning or knowledge of how to learn. For reading activities, students comprehend better if they ask themselves who, what, where, and how questions as they read. For writing activities, students do better if they ask "For whom am I writing? What is being explained? What are the steps?" And, students do better in math if they talk themselves through problem solving.

2. KEY CONCEPTS, PRINCIPLES AND THEORIES

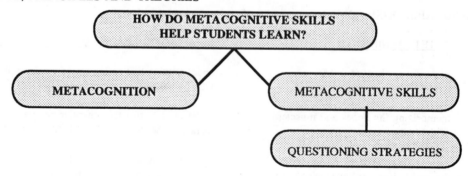

IV. WHAT STUDY STRATEGIES HELP STUDENTS LEARN?

1. SELF-CHECK ITEM: Brainstorm and list study strategies that are effective in promoting learning, then review to make sure you have included all those this section considers important. Develop a plan with steps you would use for directly teaching each strategy on your list.

TYPICAL RESPONSE: List study strategies and plan steps for teaching each.

STUDY STRATEGY	STUDY PLAN
underlining	assist student in selecting key words, phrases, or concepts
outlining	have students follow headings and subheadings of the text
summarizing	have students read a paragraph of text, then put into their own words
mapping	have students draw a concept map of a topic that is hierarchical in structure
PQ4R	Prior to reading a chapter, have students preview by skimming through the material and asking questions about concepts they might encounter. Next, have students read and, while reading, reflect, recite, and review the material.

2. KEY CONCEPTS, PRINCIPLES, AND THEORIES

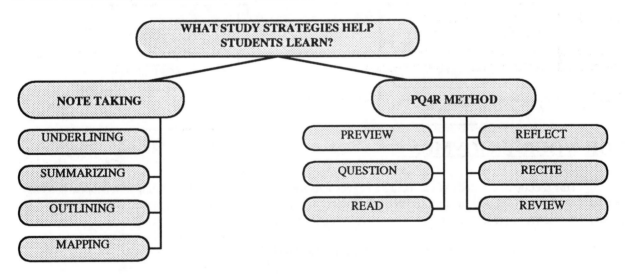

VI. HOW DO COGNITIVE TEACHING STRATEGIES HELP STUDENTS LEARN?

1. SELF-CHECK ITEM: Identify the general purpose of each set below of cognitive teaching strategies and then give a classroom example illustrating the use of each strategy. How could you illustrate all the strategies in the context of one particular lesson you might teach?
        SET 1: advance organizer, analogy, elaboration
        SET 2: questioning, conceptual model

TYPICAL RESPONSE: Identify the purpose of the above strategies and give an example of each.

The general purpose of set 1 is to activate the learner's prior knowledge before a lesson is presented. The general purpose of set 2 is to assist the learner in organizing newly learned information.

LESSON STRATEGY	EXAMPLE
advance organizer	initial statement about a subject to be learned that provides structure to the new information and relates it to information students already possess
analogy	using an example that is like the concept to be learned on one level, but unlike the concept on others
elaboration	provide a process of thinking about material to be learned in a way that connects it to information or ideas already in the learner's mind
questioning	procedure that allows students to stop instruction in order to assess their learning of the material to that point
conceptual model	an introduction of diagrams showing how elements or concepts are related

2. KEY CONCEPTS, PRINCIPLES, AND THEORIES

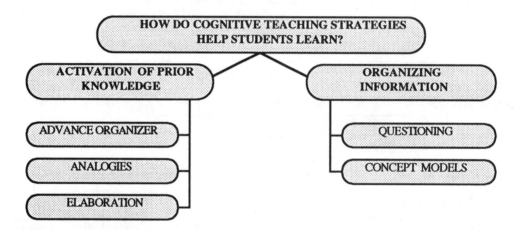

FOR YOUR ENJOYMENT

This section of the study guide includes suggestions for enriching your understanding of a chapter heading you have mastered. You will find information on activities related to the heading and suggestions for research papers, interviews, or presentations.

I. WHAT IS AN INFORMATION PROCESSING MODEL?

1. Interview several individuals about how they remember (e.g., study for an exam). Try to examine the responses from an information processing perspective.

2. For a research paper, review the research on the relationship between computers and human learning.

II. WHAT CAUSES PEOPLE TO REMEMBER OR FORGET?

1. Create a lesson plan that addresses practice; distributed, part, or enactment.

III. HOW CAN MEMORY STRATEGIES BE TAUGHT?

1. Design a lesson that requires memorization of information. Include a strategy that will enhance recall.

2. For a research paper, review the literature on memory enhancement.

IV. WHAT MAKES LEARNING MEANINGFUL?

1. Analyze a lesson from a teacher's manual. Consider the prior knowledge (e.g., facts, concepts) necessary for understanding the lesson.

2. For a research paper, review the literature on prior knowledge and its effects on new learning.

V. HOW DO METACOGNITIVE SKILLS HELP STUDENTS LEARN?

1. Select students who are at the grade level you intend to teach and interview them about their learning strategies. Analyze their responses.

VI. WHAT STUDY STRATEGIES HELP STUDENTS LEARN?

1. Interview various individuals on how they study. According to research, are their strategies useful?

2. For a research paper, review the literature on the PQ4R study strategy.

VII. HOW DO COGNITIVE TEACHING STRATEGIES HELP STUDENTS LEARN?

1. For your area, design some study skill strategies that would be helpful to your students.

CHAPTER SIX: SELF-ASSESSMENT

DIRECTIONS: Below are questions related to the main ideas presented in the chapter. Correct answers or typical responses can be found at the end of the study guide.

1. Sperling's study involving the recall of very briefly displayed letters illustrates the limitations of

   A. long term memory.
   B. short term memory.
   C. rehearsal and coding.
   D. the sensory register.

2. Match the following memory components with the characteristics that describe each.

   _____ episodic memory   A. component from which information is most easily lost

   _____ semantic memory   B. component where information is stored in schema-like networks

   _____ short term memory   C. component that represents consciousness

   _____ sensory register   D. component that stores life experiences

3. All of the following teaching strategies would be recommended for reducing retroactive inhibition EXCEPT

    A. Be consistent in the methods used when teaching similar concepts.
    B. Teach one concept thoroughly before introducing another.
    C. Use mnemonic devices to point out differences between concepts.
    D. Teach the concepts at different times, such as in separate class periods.

4. _____ A student who has trouble remembering the location of the African countries Ghana and Guinea after learning the South American country of Guyana has fallen prey to this.

    _____ A student who has trouble learning how to spell guerrilla after having earlier learned to spell gorilla is being hindered by this.

5. Using concepts in this chapter, write a well-reasoned argument supporting or refuting the claim that practice makes perfect.

6. Match the following types of learning tasks with a correct example of each.

    _____ paired associate   A. memorizing the names of the world's continents in order by size

    _____ serial   B. paraphrasing each of a series of sentences

    _____ free recall   C. memorizing the names, functions, and locations of the major organs in the human body

                                       D. learning that a group of geese is a gaggle, a group of lions is a pride, and a group of quails is a bevy

7. Refer to the scenario at the beginning of the chapter. Suppose that students could keep everything that ever entered their mind. Would they be geniuses or blithering idiots as Ms. Bishop suggests? What would their lives be like in college if they did remember everything? How about life in general?

8. Some educators argue that low achieving students should be given more training strategies than high achieving students. Some argue that more training should be given to disadvantaged students. From an information processing perspective, support or reject these arguments.

PRACTICE TEST ANSWERS

1. True; Perception is not as straightforward as reception of stimuli; rather, it is influenced by our mental state, past experiences and knowledge, motivation, and many other factors.

2. True; According to Max Wertheimer, Kurt Koffka, and Wolfgang Kohler -- three Gestalt psychologists -- we perceive whole units that add up to more than the individual parts.

3. True; Figure-ground relationship is an important principle of Gestalt psychology. It suggests that we attempt to separate what we focus on (figure) from the rest of the information presented (background).

4. Short term memory; Short term memory is a processing system that holds a limited amount of information for a few seconds (without repetition or rehearsal).

5. Long term memory; Long term memory is a storage system that can hold up to an unlimited amount of information over long periods of time.

6. B, A, C; Episodic memory stores images of events, semantic (or declarative) memory stores information of ideas, facts, or relationships, and procedural memory is a compilation of semantic information that has become automatic and non-verbal, thus requiring little processing time or space.

7. Levels of processing theory holds that people subject stimuli to different levels of mental manipulation. Only information subjected to deep level processing is retained.

8. Dual code theory hypothesizes that information that is retained in long term memory in two forms -- episodic and semantic -- is recalled more easily than information stored in one form exclusively.

9. False; Most forgetting occurs because information in short term memory is not transferred to long term memory.

10. True; Short term memory is limited in its capacity; therefore, attention to one mental task can interfere with attention to another through overloading.

11. B, C, D, A; Proactive inhibition occurs when the learning of one set of information interferes with learning of later information. Proactive facilitation occurs when learning one thing can help in learning similar, but new, information. Retroactive facilitation occurs when learning new information improves one's understanding of previously learned information. Retroactive inhibition occurs when previously learned information is lost because it is mixed up with new and somewhat similar information.

12. Primacy and recency; The tendency to learn the first things presented is called the primacy effect. The tendency to learn the last things presented is called the recency effect.

13. An example of massed practice would be "cramming" for an exam -- practicing newly learned information intensively in a short span of time. An example of distributed practice would be homework -- practicing newly learned information over an extended span of time. An example of part learning would be learning multiplication tables by 2s, the 3s, then 4s over time -- practicing information that is broken down into parts.

14. True; Students often learn things as facts before they understand concepts or skills.

15. Imagery, stimulus selection and coding, and mnemonics

16. Loci method, pegword method, Initial letter

17. Rhyming pegwords, songs, catchy phrases, initial letter strategies

18. D; Meaningful learning involves the use of old information in a non-arbitrary fashion.

19. C; Knowledge that could and should be applicable to a wide range of situations, but is only applied to a restricted set of circumstances, is called inert knowledge.

20. A; According to schema theory, information is stored in hierarchies.

21. Memorizing multiplication tables, chemical symbols for the elements, words in a foreign language, and names of the bones and muscles of the body

22. Understanding that silver is an excellent conductor of electricity -- and that silver and electricity have a relationship, but can also be considered alone.

23. Meaningful learning requires the active involvement of the learner who has a history of prior experiences and knowledge (background knowledge) to bring to understanding and incorporating new information.

24. Metacognition; Metacognition means knowing about one's learning.

25. C; Thinking skills and study skills (e.g., planning a study strategy) are metacognitive skills.

26. A; Not all students develop metacognitive skills.

27. All of the following are examples of metacognitive skills: assessing understanding, figuring out length of study time, choosing a study plan, looking for common elements in a given task, questioning, and self-talk.

28. True; Note taking research is inconsistent; however, it seems to work best with complex, conceptual materials in which the critical task is to identify main ideas.

29. False; Summarizing involves writing brief statements that represent the main ideas being read.

30. Outlining; Outlining presents the main points of the material in a hierarchical format, with each detail organized under a higher level category.

31. Mapping; Networking identifies main ideas and then makes connections between them in the form of a diagram.

32. The steps of the PQ4R method are: 1) preview; 2) question; 3) read; 4) reflect on the material; 5) recite; and 6) review.

33. B, D, C, E, A; Analogies are examples that are alike in one aspect, but otherwise are different. Elaboration means the linking of new information with prior knowledge by adding relevant or irrelevant connections. Conceptual models are diagrams showing relationships between concepts. Questioning gives students the chance to assess their understanding during the learning process. Advance organizers provide a framework for the to-be-learned material.

34. Three strategies would include: 1) using advance organizers; 2) having students discuss what they already know about the topic; and 3) asking students to predict outcomes.

35. Analogies work best when they are different from the process being explained and when the analogy is thoroughly familiar to the learner.

7
EFFECTIVE INSTRUCTION

CHAPTER OVERVIEW

The purpose of this chapter is to discuss several research-based instructional strategies that are effective in promoting student achievement. Several methods and strategies are described below.

Effective instruction includes direct instruction teaching approaches that emphasize teacher control over classroom events, including lesson presentation.

Effective instruction, from a direct instruction approach, consists of several parts including a statement of the objective(s), review of the prerequisites, presentation of the material, solicitation of student responses through guided and independent practice, assessment of performance, and distributed practice.

Effective instruction , from a direct instruction approach, has advantages and disadvantages, when compared with other instructional methods.

Effective instruction methods help students learn and transfer concepts.

Effective instruction makes use of whole group and small group discussion strategies.

CHAPTER OUTLINE

I. WHAT IS DIRECT INSTRUCTION?

II. HOW IS A DIRECT INSTRUCTION LESSON TAUGHT?
    A. State Learning Objectives
    B. Orient Students to the Lesson
    C. Review Prerequisites
    D. Present New Material
    E. Conduct Learning Probes
    F. Provide Independent Practice
    G. Assess Performance and Provide Feedback
    H. Provide Distributed Practice and Review

III. WHAT DOES RESEARCH ON DIRECT INSTRUCTION METHODS SUGGEST?
    A. Advantages and Limitations of Direct Instruction

IV. HOW DO STUDENTS LEARN AND TRANSFER CONCEPTS?
    A. Concept Learning and Teaching
    B. Teaching for Transfer of Learning

V. HOW ARE DISCUSSIONS USED IN INSTRUCTION?
    A. Subjective and Controversial Subjects
    B. Difficult and Novel Concepts
    C. Affective Objectives
    D. Whole Class Discussion
    E. Small Group Discussion

PRACTICE TEST

DIRECTIONS: Each chapter heading from the text listed below is followed by a series of related questions worth a total of ten points. Respond to each question, check your answers with those found at the end of the study guide chapter, then determine your score. Consider nine points per heading to be mastery.

For those headings on which you do not score at least nine points, turn to the FOR YOUR INFORMATION section of the study guide for corrective instruction. For those headings on which you do score at least nine points, turn to the FOR YOUR ENJOYMENT section of the study guide for enrichment activities.

I. WHAT IS DIRECT INSTRUCTION?

True and False

1. (1 point) _____ The term "direct instruction" is used to describe lessons in which the teacher transmits information directly to students, structuring class time to reach a clearly defined set of objectives as efficiently as possible.

2. (1 point) _____ Direct instruction is appropriate when exploration, discovery, and open-ended objectives drive the lesson.

Short Answer/Essay

3. (8 points) List the eight events (phases) of instruction designed by Gagne.

_____   _____

_____   _____

_____   _____

_____   _____

II. HOW IS A DIRECT INSTRUCTION LESSON TAUGHT?

True or False

4. (1 point) _____ The sequence of activities included in an effective lesson varies according to the grade level of the students.

5. (1 point) _____ The sequence of activities included in an effective lesson varies according to the subject matter content.

6. (8 points)   *Order in Sequence*

_____ Provide distributed practice.
_____ Review prerequisites.
_____ Conduct learning probes.
_____ State learning objective(s).
_____ Provide independent practice.
_____ Present new material.
_____ Assess performance and provide feedback.
_____ Orient students to lesson.

III. WHAT DOES RESEARCH ON DIRECT INSTRUCTION METHODS SUGGEST?

Sentence Completion

7. (1 point) _____ Direct instruction models based on the practices of the most effective teachers are called ___.

8. (1 point) _____ Direct instruction models based on well-structured and highly organized planning, including the motivation of students and the management of classrooms, are called ___.

9. (1 point) _____ The term used by Madeline Hunter to describe a method for stimulating students' interest is ___.

Multiple Choice

10. (1 point) _____ Research on Madeline Hunter's mastery teaching program suggests that it is

A. superior to other direct instruction programs at all grade levels and across disciplines.
B. no more and no less effective than other direct instruction program.
C. inferior to other direct instruction programs.

11. (1 point) _____ Which of the following research findings is accurate regarding the systematic instruction program called DISTAR?

A. DISTAR was least effective in increasing students' reading and math achievement when compared to other systematic instruction models.
B. DISTAR increased students' academic achievement, but had no effect on students' self-esteem.
C. DISTAR brought low achieving, disadvantaged students to nearly average.

Short Answer/Essay

12. (2 points) List two advantages of direct instruction.

_____

_____

13. (3 points) List three limitations of direct instruction.

_____

_____

_____

IV. HOW DO STUDENTS LEARN AND TRANSFER CONCEPTS?

True or False

14. (1 point) _____ A concept is a category under which specific elements may be grouped.

15. (1 point) _____ With a rule-example-rule approach to concept learning, teachers give students instances of the concept, then ask them to provide a definition.

16. (1 point) _____ Transfer of learning depends on the degree of similarity between the learning situation and the situation to which it is to be applied.

17. (1 point) _____ If a student learns a skill or concept in one domain, it can be assumed that the knowledge will transfer to another domain.

18. (3 points)

Short Answer/Essay
List the three rules to follow when presenting examples of concepts.

_____

_____

_____

19. (3 points) Describe the difference in strategies between teaching for transfer and teaching initial learning.

_____

_____

IV. HOW ARE DISCUSSIONS USED IN INSTRUCTION?

20. (3 points)

Short Answer/Essay
List three types of learning objectives that are best met by using discussions.

_____

_____

_____

21. (1 point) Define "inquiry oriented discussion."

_____

22. (1 point) Define "exploring points of view."

_____

23. (2 points) List two functions of the teacher when using whole class discussion.

_____

_____

24. (3 points) Explain the roles of the teacher, the group leader, and the group secretary when using small group discussion.

_____

SCORING	POINTS NEEDED FOR MASTERY	POINTS RECEIVED
I. WHAT IS DIRECT INSTRUCTION?	9	
II. HOW IS A DIRECT INSTRUCTION LESSON TAUGHT?	9	
III. WHAT DOES RESEARCH ON DIRECT INSTRUCTION SUGGEST?	9	
IV. HOW DO STUDENTS LEARN AND TRANSFER CONCEPTS?	9	
V. HOW ARE DISCUSSIONS USED IN INSTRUCTION?	9	

FOR YOUR INFORMATION

This section of the study guide includes suggestions for further study of the information you have not yet mastered. You will find information on: 1) typical responses to the SELF-CHECK item(s) from the text; and 2) key concepts, principles, and theories addressed in the text chapter.

I. WHAT IS AN EFFECTIVE LESSON?

1. SELF-CHECK ITEM: List the sequence of seven steps in presenting a direct instruction lesson, leaving space below each step for adding information later.

TYPICAL RESPONSE: List the steps in a direction instruction lesson.

1. State the learning objective and orient students to the lesson.
2. Review the prerequisites.
3. Present new material.
4. Conduct learning probes.
5. Provide independent practice.
6. Assess students' performance and provide feedback.
7. Provide distributed practice and review.

2. KEY CONCEPTS, PRINCIPLES, AND THEORIES

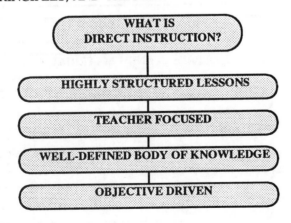

WHAT IS DIRECT INSTRUCTION?

HIGHLY STRUCTURED LESSONS

TEACHER FOCUSED

WELL-DEFINED BODY OF KNOWLEDGE

OBJECTIVE DRIVEN

II. HOW IS A DIRECT INSTRUCTION LESSON TAUGHT?

1. SELF-CHECK ITEM: Continue the list you began in the previous section by adding information about each step of a direct instruction lesson. Add information for the following categories: purpose, strategy, example.

TYPICAL RESPONSE: Add information to the steps of a direct instruction lesson.

1. State the learning objective and orient students to lesson.
   PURPOSE: inform students of lesson purpose, establish attitude, arouse curiosity
   STRATEGY: state as specific change in behavior, skill performance level, attitude; pose questions
   EXAMPLE: "After the lesson you will be able to . . ." or "Have you ever wondered why . . . "
2. Review the prerequisites.
   PURPOSE: access prior knowledge
   STRATEGY: review material learned previously
   EXAMPLE: "Yesterday we learned . . ."
3. Present new material.
   PURPOSE: present new information or skills
   STRATEGY: organize logically, clearly; explain and demonstrate
   EXAMPLE: "The lesson for today is about . . ."
4. Conduct learning probe.
   PURPOSE: access students' understanding of new material
   STRATEGY: questioning -- written, physical, or oral
   EXAMPLE: "Let's review what has been discussed . . ."
5. Provide independent practice.
   PURPOSE: practice using newly learned concepts
   STRATEGY: seatwork, monitored by teacher
   EXAMPLE: "Work on questions 1 -10 . . ."
6. Assess performance and provide feedback.
   PURPOSE: determine if students have mastered the objective
   STRATEGY: ranges from informal questioning to formal written exam
   EXAMPLE: "You will take a short quiz . . . "
7. Provide distributed practice and review.
   PURPOSE: practice newly learned concepts independently
   STRATEGY: homework
   EXAMPLE: "By tomorrow, complete the following . . . "

2. KEY CONCEPTS, PRINCIPLES, AND THEORIES

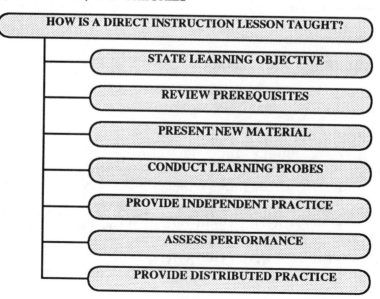

III. WHAT DOES RESEARCH ON DIRECT INSTRUCTION SUGGEST?

1. SELF-CHECK ITEM: List three variants of the direct instruction method. What does research suggest about the effectiveness of these teaching models?

TYPICAL RESPONSE: Describe variants of direct instruction and discuss research findings.

Hunter Mastery Program:	Hunter's program provides a general guide to effective lessons in any subject or grade level. Segments include: 1) getting started, 2) input and modeling, 3) checking for understanding, and 4) independent practice. Research on the effectiveness of the Hunter program is mixed.
Missouri Math Program:	The Missouri math program originates from research conducted on effective teachers and less effective teachers. The principle features include: 1) opening, 2) development, 3) seatwork, 4) homework, and 5) special review. Research shows that the Missouri math program students gained somewhat more in math knowledge than students in a control group.
Systematic Instruction Models:	Systematic instruction models are highly structured, direct instruction programs. Some (e.g., DISTAR, Behavior Analysis) have shown improvements in academic achievement in math for disadvantaged, low achieving students.

2. KEY CONCEPTS, PRINCIPLES, AND THEORIES

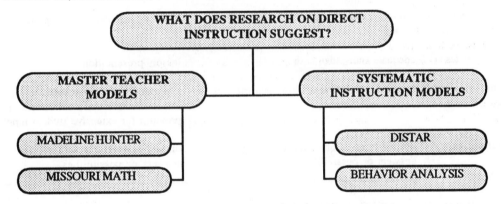

IV. HOW DO STUDENTS LEARN AND TRANSFER CONCEPTS?

1. SELF-CHECK ITEM: Construct an example showing how you would use the following approaches to teach your students a concept: rule-example-rule and examples/non-examples. Explain how to teach students to transfer concepts.

TYPICAL RESPONSE: Construct examples of rule-example-rule and examples/non-examples teaching.

rule-example-rule approach:	state a definition, present several instances of the definition, then restate the definition and show how the instances typify the definition
examples and non-examples:	order the examples from easy to difficult, select examples that differ from one another, then, compare and contrast examples and non-examples

2. KEY CONCEPTS, PRINCIPLES, AND THEORIES

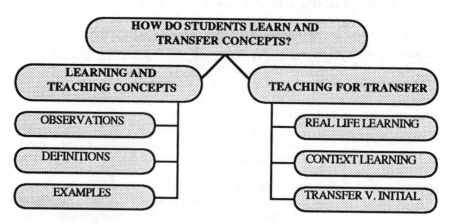

V. HOW ARE DISCUSSIONS USED IN INSTRUCTION?

1. SELF-CHECK ITEM: Create a two-column chart comparing and contrasting whole group and small group discussion in terms of the following categories: appropriate uses, prerequisites, benefits, and limitations.

TYPICAL RESPONSE: Create a chart about whole group and small group discussion.

	WHOLE GROUP DISCUSSION	SMALL GROUP DISCUSSION
appropriate uses	inquiry training, exploring points of view	discuss particular topic or parts of topic
prerequisites	adequate knowledge base	lesson presentation
benefits	exploration of diverse views and theories	exploration of diverse views and theories (most effective when controversy is explored) provides for extensive student input
limitations	limited to questions with multiple answers or possibilities	limited to questions with multiple answers or possibilities

2. KEY CONCEPTS, PRINCIPLES, AND THEORIES

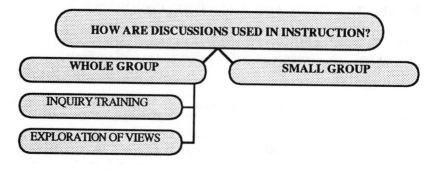

FOR YOUR ENJOYMENT

This section of the study guide includes suggestions for enriching your understanding of a chapter heading you have mastered. You will find information on activities related to the heading and suggestions for research papers, interviews, or presentation.

I. WHAT IS DIRECT INSTRUCTION?

1. In your own classes, identify the elements of direct instruction you observe.

2. Review teacher manuals. Select several examples of direct instruction approaches.

II. HOW IS A DIRECT INSTRUCTION LESSON TAUGHT?

1. Review the variants of direct instruction (e.g., Gagne, Slavin, Hunter). Discuss the advantages and disadvantages of each. Select the one that best fits you.

2. Design a lesson using a direct instruction approach.

III. WHAT DOES RESEARCH ON DIRECT INSTRUCTION SUGGEST?

1. For a research paper, review the literature on the effectiveness of direct instruction.

IV. HOW DO STUDENTS LEARN AND TRANSFER CONCEPTS?

1. For a research paper, review the literature on teaching for transfer.

V. HOW ARE DISCUSSIONS USED IN INSTRUCTION?

1. Make a list of open-ended or controversial discussion questions appropriate for your area of study.

CHAPTER SEVEN: SELF-ASSESSMENT

DIRECTIONS: Below are questions related to the main ideas presented in the chapter. Correct answers or typical responses can be found at the end of the study guide.

1. All of the following terms describe effective instruction EXCEPT

   A. immediate feedback.
   B. clear goals.
   C. frequent monitoring of performance.
   D. learner control.
   E. structured interactions.

2. The seven steps in a direct instruction lesson are listed below in alphabetical order. Rearrange the steps in the order in which they should occur.

   A. Assess performance and provide feedback.
   B. Conduct learning probes.
   C. Present new material.
   D. Provide distributed practice and review.
   E. Provide independent practice.
   F. Review prerequisites.
   G. State learning objects and orient students to lesson.

3.   Research suggests that direct instruction methods work best in all of the following contexts EXCEPT

   A. teaching basic skills.
   B. elementary reading.
   C. teaching low achievers and at risk students.
   D. teaching critical thinking skills.

4.   Which of the following conclusions is supported by research?

   A. Give low achievers as much time to respond as high achievers.
   B. Call on another student if a student doesn't answer quickly, to avoid embarrassment.
   C. Call on volunteers rather than selecting students in a prescribed order.
   D. Encourage choral responses when questions have more than one possible answer.
   E. Call on students randomly and then ask questions aloud.

5.   Which of the following situations best illustrates transfer of learning?

   A. Students who carefully study the week's material do well on the quiz.
   B. Students use their knowledge of geometry to solve a perspectives problem in art.
   C. Students rehearse a scene from an Ionesco play after memorizing the lines.
   D. Students correctly identify an example of a concept being taught.

6.   Refer to the chapter opening scenario. Although Ms. Logan's approach seems to be effective, she appears exhausted. What are the costs and benefits of the teaching method she uses and of other teaching approaches (e.g., discovery learning, direct instruction, discussion)?

7.   How would you deal with the following situations in a whole class discussion?

   A. a student who never makes a comment
   B. a student who talks more than anyone else
   C. two students who begin arguing
   D. a student who interrupts another student

PRACTICE TEST ANSWERS

1. True; Direct instruction involves teacher-directed activities based on specific objectives.

2. False; Direct instruction is appropriate when teaching a well-defined body of information or skills.

3. Motivation, apprehending, acquisition, retention, recall, generalization, performance, feedback

4. False; The sequence of activities included in an effective lesson does not vary by grade level.

5. False; The sequence of activities included in an effective lesson does not vary by subject.

6. State learning objective. Orient students to lesson. Review prerequisites. Present new material. Conduct learning probes. Provide independent practice. Assess performance and provide feedback. Provide distributed practice and review.

7. Master teacher models; This category includes Madeline Hunter's mastery teaching and the Missouri math program.

8. Systematic instruction models. These are similar to the mastery teaching models. They are highly structured and inclusive of non-academic events.

9. Anticipatory set; An anticipatory set is created in students by focusing their attention on the material to be presented, reminding them of what they already know and stimulating their interest in the lesson.

10. B; Despite widespread popularity, evaluations of Hunter's mastery teaching program have not generally found that the students of teachers trained in the model have learned more than other students.

11. C; DISTAR increased the academic achievement levels of disadvantaged low achievers.

12. One advantage of direct instruction is that it can improve the teaching of basic skills. A second advantage is that it is a structured, systematic instructional program.

13. One limitation of direct instruction is that, to date, research has focused on reading and math, but not on other subjects. A second limitation is that it is sometimes uncritically applied to educational settings with the belief that changes will occur. A final limitation is that there is not enough research at the secondary level.

14. True; A concept is a category under which specific elements may be grouped.

15. False; A rule-example-rule approach gives students a definition, then asks students to consider examples and non-examples.

16. True; Transfer of knowledge from one domain to another is dependent upon the similarity between the two.

17. False; It can never be assumed that transfer of learning has occurred.

18. The three rules are: 1) order the examples from easy to difficult; 2) select examples that differ from one another; and 3) compare and contrast examples and non-examples.

19. Teaching for transfer requires the ability to apply knowledge to a variety of circumstances; therefore, similar examples, less similar examples, and non-examples are used to facilitate the process. Initial learning requires that

very similar examples be used.

20. Learning objectives that work best for discussion: focus on content without simple answers, contain difficult concepts that challenge misconceptions and are affective in nature.

21. Inquiry training involves presenting students with a puzzling event or experiment that they must solve through theory generation and hypothesis testing.

22. Exploring points of view involves asking students to explore ideas and develop their own beliefs about newly learned information.

23. One teacher function is to guide the discussion. A second function is to help the class avoid dead ends.

24. The teacher prepares the students (with lessons and clear instructions about the group's task). The group leader keeps the group on task and ensures that all group members participate. The group secretary records the group's ideas.

8
STUDENT-CENTERED AND CONSTRUCTIVIST APPROACHES TO INSTRUCTION

CHAPTER OVERVIEW

The purpose of this chapter is to discuss several student-centered and constructivist approaches to instruction. Several main points from the chapter are listed below.

Student-centered and constructivist approaches to instruction include cooperative, generative, discovery, and self-regulated learning.

Student-centered and constructivist approaches to instruction include several cooperative learning approaches, including team assisted individualization, student teams-achievement division, cooperative integrated reading and composition, jigsaw, learning together, and group investigation.

Student-centered and constructivist approaches to instruction emphasize creative problem solving and critical thinking skills.

CHAPTER OUTLINE

I. WHAT IS THE CONSTRUCTIVIST VIEW OF LEARNING?
    A. Historical Roots of Constructivism
    B. Top Down Processing
    C. Cooperative Learning
    D. Generative Learning
    E. Discovery Learning
    F. Self-Regulated Learning
    G. Scaffolding
    H. APA's Learner-Centered Psychological Principles
    I. Constructivist Methods in the Content Areas
    J. Research on Constructivist Methods

II. HOW IS COOPERATIVE LEARNING USED IN INSTRUCTION?
    A. Cooperative Learning Methods
    B. Research on Cooperative Learning

III. HOW ARE PROBLEM AND THINKING SKILLS TAUGHT?
    A. Steps in the Problem Solving Process
    B. Obstacles to Problem Solving
    C. Teaching Creative Problem Solving
    D. Teaching Thinking Skills
    E. Critical Thinking

PRACTICE TEST

DIRECTIONS: Each chapter heading from the text listed below is followed by a series of related questions worth a total of ten points. Respond to each question, check your answers with those found at the end of the study guide chapter, then determine your score. Consider nine points per heading to be mastery.

For those headings on which you do not score at least nine points, turn to the FOR YOUR INFORMATION section of the study guide for corrective instruction. For those headings on which you do score at least nine points, turn to the FOR YOUR ENJOYMENT section of the study guide for enrichment activities.

I. WHAT IS A CONSTRUCTIVIST VIEW OF LEARNING?

True or False

1. (1 point) _____ The main point of constructivist theory is that learners must individually discover and transform complex information if they are to make it their own.

2. (1 point) _____ Constructivist theory draws heavily on the work of Vygotsky and Piaget.

3. (1 point) _____ Constructivists advocate discovery learning.

Multiple Choice

4. (1 point) _____ All of the following explanations address the connection between constructivist approaches and cooperative learning EXCEPT:
   A. The combination emphasizes the social nature of learning .
   B. The combination uses peers to model appropriate ways of thinking.
   C. The combination allows for students' basic knowledge to become complex knowledge.
   D. The combination requires students to challenge their misconceptions.

Short Answer/Essay

5. (2 points) List two ways in which students can be taught "generative" learning.

   _____

   _____

6. (4 points) List two advantages of discovery learning and explain why they are advantages.

   _____

   _____

   _____

   _____

II. HOW IS COOPERATIVE LEARNING USED IN INSTRUCTION?

True or False

7. (1 point) _____ Cooperative learning refers to instructional methods in which students work together in small groups in order to help each other learn.

8. (1 point) _____ Research indicates that cooperative learning is effective in grades two through 12 in all subjects.

9. (2 points)   *Short Answer/Essay*
List the two conditions necessary for student achievement when a cooperative learning approach is used.

_____

_____

10. (6 points)   List the characteristics associated with jigsaw, learning together, and group investigation.

_____

_____

_____

III. HOW ARE PROBLEM SOLVING AND THINKING SKILLS TAUGHT?

11. (1 point)   _____   *True or False*
Problem solving abilities are innate and, therefore, cannot be taught.

12. (1 point)   _____   One indication of transfer of learning is the ability to use information and solve problems.

13. (1 point)   _____   *Sentence Completion*
The term used to describe how individuals fail to see new problem solving alternatives because they are locked into the conventional is ___.

14. (3 points)   *Short Answer/Essay*
Briefly describe the following problem solving steps: means-ends analysis, extracting relevant information, and representing the problem.

_____

_____

_____

15. (4 points)   List the steps necessary for creative problem solving.

_____

_____

_____

_____

SCORING	POINTS NEEDED FOR MASTERY	POINTS RECEIVED
I. WHAT IS THE CONSTRUCTIVIST VIEW OF LEARNING?	9	
II. HOW IS COOPERATIE LEARNING USED IN INSTRUCTION?	9	
III. HOW ARE PROBLEM SOLVING AND THINKING SKILLS TAUGHT?	9	

FOR YOUR INFORMATION

This section of the study guide includes suggestions for further study of the information you have not yet mastered. You will find information on: 1) typical responses to the SELF-CHECK item(s) from the text; and 2) key concepts, principles, and theories addressed in the text chapter.

I. WHAT IS THE CONSTRUCTIVIST VIEW OF LEARNING?

1. SELF-CHECK ITEM: Write a short essay explaining how each of the following terms is related to constructivist theory: top down processing, generative learning, discovery learning, self-regulated learning, and scaffolding.

TYPICAL RESPONSE: Write a short essay using key terms.

> A revolution known as "constructivism" is taking place in educational psychology. It builds on Piagetian and Vygotskian concepts of learning -- that learners must be active and that learning must involve *discovery* and inquiry and relate to the real world. Constructivism is a *top down approach* in which complex problem solving leads to the learning of basic skills. Since *discovery* is involved in constructivist approaches, *generative techniques* such as students writing questions, summaries, or analogies following a learning experience are encouraged. Constructivism creates *self-regulated learning* because students are required to be knowledgeable about effective learning strategies and know when to use them.

2. KEY CONCEPTS, PRINCIPLES, AND THEORIES

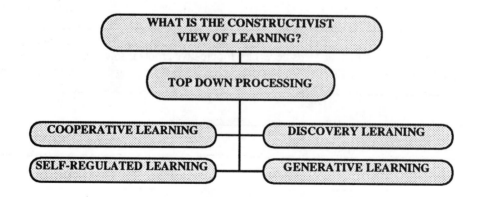

II. HOW IS COOPERATIVE LEARNING USED IN INSTRUCTION?

1. SELF-CHECK ITEM: List at least three specific benefits of cooperative learning that research findings confirm and explain how you would go about introducing STAD in your classroom.

TYPICAL RESPONSE: List the benefits of cooperative learning.

> 1. Students learn substantially more in cooperative groups if they are rewarded and if the success of the group is dependent upon each individual.
> 2. Cooperative learning methods can have a positive effect on race relations, self-esteem, attitude toward school, and acceptance of students with special needs.
> 3. Students learn to work together using active listening, giving good explanations, avoiding putdowns, and involving others.

TYPICAL RESPONSE: How would you introduce STAD to your class?

> 1. Assign students to teams (four or five students of mixed abilities).
> 2. Make a worksheet and a short quiz for the lesson. Have the team study the material.
> 3. Distribute the quiz and have students complete it independently.
> 4. Figure individual and team scores.
> 5. Recognize team accomplishments.

2. KEY CONCEPTS, PRINCIPLES, AND THEORIES

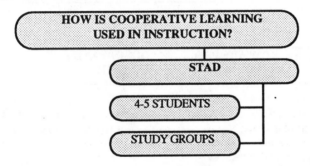

III: HOW ARE PROBLEM SOLVING AND THINKING SKILLS TAUGHT?

1. SELF-CHECK ITEM: Explain how you would apply the following techniques to solve the problem below: means-ends analysis, extracting relevant information, overcoming functional fixedness, identifying assumptions, thinking divergently, and representing the problem.

> *Two buses at stations 100 miles apart leave their respective stations at precisely 2:00 pm and drive toward each other at an average speed of 50 miles per hour. At the same moment, a small plane at station A takes flight and flies 100 miles per hour back and fourth two times between the two oncoming buses. How many miles will the plane have flown by the time the two buses meet?*

TYPICAL RESPONSE: Apply the learning techniques to the math problem.

TECHNIQUE	EXPLANATION
means-ends analysis:	(involves what the problem is and what needs to be done) This is a math problem involving time and distance.
extracting relevant information:	(involves being able to select relevant information while ignoring the irrelevant)

It is necessary to know the speed and distance traveled by each bus and the plane. "On the average" is important. Knowing that the plane flies back and fourth two times is irrelevant. Knowing that the buses leave together is important; however, the fact that it is 2:00 pm is unimportant.

overcoming functional fixedness:	(problem solving block when one cannot consider beyond the conventional) Perhaps believing that the problem can be solved at all!
identifying assumptions:	(identifying misleading and conflicting evidence) It cannot be assumed that two buses traveling "on the average" of 50 miles per hour is the same as two buses traveling consistently at 50 miles per hour. It cannot be assumed that a bus left from Station A as the plane did. It could be that Station A for the plane is far away from the buses.
divergent thinking:	(accepting other viewpoints as legitimate) One divergent view is that the problem is stated in such a way that it could be solved (the answer being 50 miles); however, too many "holes" exist (see identifying assumptions) in the information to say it can be solved with certainty.
representing the problem:	(seeing the problem accurately) While it seems like a straightforward distance and time problem, it is not.

2. KEY CONCEPTS, PRINCIPLES, AND THEORIES

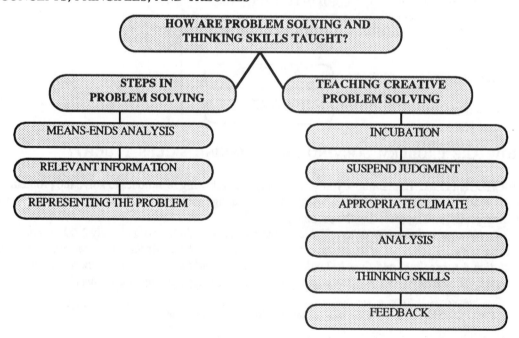

FOR YOUR ENJOYMENT

This section of the study guide includes suggestions for enriching your understanding of a chapter heading you have mastered. You will find information on activities related to the heading and suggestions for research papers, interviews, or presentations.

I. WHAT IS THE CONSTRUCTIVIST VIEW OF LEARNING?

1. For a research paper, review the literature on constructivism.

2. Create lessons using a discovery approach.

II. HOW IS COOPERATIVE LEARNING USED IN INSTRUCTION?

1. For a research paper, review the literature on cooperative learning.

III. HOW ARE PROBLEM SOLVING AND THINKING SKILLS TAUGHT?

1. Design a lesson that enhances problem solving skills.

2. For a research paper, review the literature on problem solving.

CHAPTER EIGHT: SELF-ASSESSMENT

DIRECTIONS: Below are questions related to the main ideas presented in the chapter. Correct answers or typical responses can be found at the end of the study guide.

1. In assisted or mediated learning, the teacher

    A. lets students explore topics to further their learning.
    B. presents information in a structured lesson.
    C. guides instruction so that students acquire learning tools.
    D. gives instruction in basic skills.

2. All of the following strategies reflect a constructivist view of learning EXCEPT

    A. self monitoring.
    B. social learning.
    C. bottom-up processing.
    D. discovery learning.

3. Define discovery learning, self-regulated learning, and scaffolding. Give an example of each.

4. Research suggests that cooperative learning programs, such as STAD, are effective in all of the following conditions EXCEPT

    A. Groups receive rewards or recognition for achievement.
    B. Groups are mixed in terms of race, ethnicity, gender, and special needs.
    C. The success of the group depends on the individual learning of each group member.
    D. Students are grouped together by ability.
    E. Groups work together for discovery, discussion, and study.

5. Problem solving may require all of the following skills EXCEPT

    A. critical thinking.
    B. divergent thinking.
    C. functional fixedness.
    D. brainstorming.

6.   Refer to the scenario at the beginning of the chapter. What are some of the constructivist learning principles that are used? What is the constructivist view of learning?

7.   Describe an example of discovery learning. Explain your role as a teacher in it. Explain a weakness and a strength of this type of learning.

8.   Assume that one of your goals is to improve your students' creative problem solving abilities. What might be possible interferences to their problem solving? What are ways in which you can facilitate problem solving?

PRACTICE TEST ANSWERS

1. True; Constructivists believe learners must transform knowledge in order to make it their own.

2. True; The historical roots of constructivist theory are with Piaget and Vygotsky.

3. True; Constructivists, like Piaget, Vygotsky, and Bruner, advocate discovery learning.

4. C; Constructivist approaches begin with the discovery of basic skills through complex problem solving.

5. Students can make up their own questions, write summaries from lectures, or create analogies.

6. Discovery learning arouses students' curiosity, which motivates them to continue working until they find answers. Discovery learning develops problem solving skills and critical thinking because students must analyze and manipulate information.

7. True; Cooperative learning generally refers to groups of four learners who are of mixed abilities.

8. True; Cooperative learning research has found it to be an effective method of instruction.

9. First, there must be some reward or recognition. Second, the success of the group must depend on the individual learning of each group member.

10. Jigsaw groups form teams of experts on a section of the to-be-learned material who teach non-experts. Learning together groups hand in a single completed assignment. Group investigation groups use inquiry, discussion, and cooperative planning and projects.

11. False; Problem solving is a skill that can be taught and learned.

12. True; Transfer of learning requires problem solving skills.

13. Functional fixedness

14. Means-ends analysis involves deciding what the problem is and what needs to be done. Extracting relevant information means selecting the segments of the problem that contain important information while ignoring other information. Representing the problem accurately is essential in order to solve the problem.

15. The steps necessary for creative problem solving include: incubation, suspension of judgment, establishment of appropriate climate, and analysis.

9
ACCOMMODATING INSTRUCTION TO MEET INDIVIDUAL NEEDS

CHAPTER OVERVIEW

In previous chapters, behavioral and cognitive theories of learning and research on effective instruction were discussed. This chapter shows how instruction is adapted in the classroom to enhance learning. Some of the most effective instructional strategies used to accommodate instruction to individual needs are listed below.

Accommodating instruction to meet individual needs is a product of quality instruction, taught at the appropriate level, with adequate incentives and time to learn.

Accommodating instruction to meet individual needs includes the use of within-class ability grouping in which students form mixed ability cooperative learning teams that do not segregate lower achievers from their classmates.

Accommodating instruction to meet individual needs includes the use of mastery learning where a preestablished mastery criterion is identified along with opportunities for correction when the criterion is not met and enrichment when it is met.

Accommodating instruction to meet individual needs includes the use of individualized learning strategies -- often seen as computer based instruction and cross-age or adult one-on-one tutors -- to address learning differences.

CHAPTER OUTLINE

I. WHAT ARE ELEMENTS OF EFFECTIVE INSTRUCTION BEYOND A GOOD LESSON?
   A. Carroll's Model of School Learning and QAIT

II. HOW ARE STUDENTS GROUPED TO ACCOMMODATE ACHIEVEMENT?
   A. Between-Class Ability Grouping
   B. Untracking
   C. Regrouping for Reading and Mathematics
   D. Nongraded (Cross-Age Grouping) Elementary Schools
   E. Within-Class Ability Grouping

III. WHAT IS MASTERY LEARNING?
   A. Forms of Mastery Learning
   B. How Mastery Learning Works
   C. Research on Mastery Learning
   D. Outcome Based Education

IV. WHAT ARE SOME WAYS OF INDIVIDUALIZING INSTRUCTION?
   A. Peer Tutoring
   B. Adult Tutoring
   C. Programmed Instruction
   D. Informal Remediation and Enrichment
   E. Computer Based Instruction

V. WHAT EDUCATION PROGRAMS EXIST FOR STUDENTS PLACED AT RISK?
  A. Compensatory Education Programs
  B. Early Intervention Programs

PRACTICE TEST

DIRECTIONS: Each chapter heading from the text listed below is followed by a series of related questions worth a total of ten points. Respond to each question, check your answers with those found at the end of the study guide chapter, then determine your score. Consider nine points per heading to be mastery.

For those headings on which you do not score at least nine points, turn to the FOR YOUR INFORMATION section of the study guide for corrective instruction. For those headings on which you do score at least nine points, turn to the FOR YOUR ENJOYMENT section for enrichment activities.

I. WHAT ARE ELEMENTS OF EFFECTIVE INSTRUCTION BEYOND A GOOD LESSON?

Multiple Choice

1. (1 point) _____ All of the following elements are necessary for effective instruction EXCEPT

A. high quality, developmentally appropriate lessons.
B. adequate incentives for students to learn.
C. appropriate amounts of time for students to learn.
D. whole group, teacher-led activities.

2. (1 point) _____ Which statement best depicts Carroll's model of effective instruction?

A. Learning is the product of aptitude and ability.
B. Achievement refers to the time needed to learn in relation to the time actually spent learning.
C. Learning is primarily a measure of the quality of instruction.
D. A learner's aptitude restricts the amount of information that he or she is capable of learning.

3. (1 point) _____ According to Carroll, which one of the following learning elements is under the direct control of the student?

A. time to learn
B. quality of instruction
D. aptitude to learn
D. level of instruction

4. (1 point) _____ A teacher blends her strong knowledge of the content with appropriate teaching strategies, at a developmentally appropriate level, and provides students with adequate practice time for learning. Which part of the QAIT model of effective instruction remains for the teacher to address?

A. perseverance
B. quality of instruction
C. incentive
D. opportunity

123

5. (4 points)

Matching

_____ A teacher designs her lessons with consideration to the students' prior knowledge and current ability.

A. quality of instruction

B. appropriate level of instruction

_____ A teacher gives recognition to students who work diligently to learn the presented material.

C. incentive

_____ A teacher creates lessons that will be interesting, informative, well-organized, and clear to students.

D. time

_____ A teacher recognizes that not all students will complete assignments simultaneously.

6. (2 points)

Short Answer/Essay

Explain the difference between student-controlled elements (from Carroll's model) and teacher-controlled elements (from the QAIT model) that guide effective instruction.

_____

_____

II. HOW ARE STUDENTS GROUPED TO ACCOMMODATE ACHIEVEMENT DIFFERENCES?

Multiple Choice

7. (1 point)   _____   Which example best describes between-class ability grouping?

A. A second grade teacher divides his class into the yellow, blue, and green math groups.
B. Following a math placement test for ninth graders, students with low scores are assigned to remedial math, students with average scores are assigned to pre-algebra, and students with high scores are assigned to algebra I.
C. A teacher's fifth grade class is made up of three cooperative learning groups, each having an equal number of high, mid, and low achievers.
D. Secondary students are allowed to choose courses from a variety of electives and are then assigned to the choices.

8. (1 point)   _____   Which example best describes within-class ability grouping?

A. From scores received on an aptitude test, a counselor assigns tenth grade students to either a college preparatory or a general education track.
B. An elementary school groups its students according to their reading level, not their grade level, so that like-ability students are together in a room for reading instruction.
C. Gifted learners from a middle school are brought together for two hours each week for additional science and math instruction.
D. A teacher assigns her students to class teams, each consisting of mixed abilities, where students work on reading vocabulary.

9. (1 point) _____ Research shows that all of the following statements are true for between-class ability grouping EXCEPT

A. Between-class ability grouping is more advantageous for low-track class members than for high-track class members.
B. A problem with between-class ability grouping is that placement in a group is often made on the basis of standardized test scores, not course achievement.
C. Placing low-achieving students together in one group decreases the possibility that they will be exposed to positive role models.
D. Teachers assigned to work with low-track classes exhibit less enthusiasm and organization than teachers assigned to work with high-track classes.

10. (1 points) _____ Which of the following is a true statement regarding effective within-class grouping, according to the research presented in the text?

A. Students of all achievement levels benefit from within-class ability groups.
B. Teachers' expectations of advanced students are lower in homogeneous ability groups than in heterogeneous ability groups.
C. Within-class ability groups have stigmatizing effects on low-achievers.

Short Answer/Essay

11. (6 points) List three types of between-class ability grouping strategies and three types of within-class ability grouping strategies used in reading or mathematics.

_____

_____

_____

III. WHAT IS MASTERY LEARNING?

True or False

12. (1 point) _____ One widely used means of adapting instruction to the needs of diverse students is called mastery learning.

Multiple Choice

13. (1 point) _____ Which statement best describes the basic underlying idea of mastery learning?

A. Making academic comparisons between students fosters healthy competition.
B. Grading on the curve is the best approach to assessing student achievement.
C. Whole group instruction that focuses mainly on low achieving students will assure that all students grasp lesson concepts.
D. Students should possess prerequisite skills prior to addressing more advanced skills, regardless of the time it takes to learn the prerequisite skill.

14. (1 point) _____ What is the term used to describe a preestablished standard that a student is required to meet in order to be considered proficient in a skill?

A. mastery criterion
B. remediation
C. enrichment

125

15. (1 point) _____ An instructional event that helps to broaden the knowledge level of students who have reached mastery level for a given outcome is called

A. an achievement test.
B. a corrective lesson.
C. an enrichment activity.

16. (1 point) _____ What is the term used to describe an instructional event that helps a student to reach mastery level when he or she was unable to do so initially?

A. achievement outcome
B. corrective instruction
C. enrichment activity
D. summative evaluation

17. (1 point) _____ Students in a high school psychology course read each chapter of the text and, when ready, take a test on the material read. If a student receives the minimum score necessary for passing, he or she proceeds to the next chapter. If a student receives less than the minimum score, he or she rereads the chapter and retakes the test until the minimum score is reached. What type of mastery learning format is in use?

A. Keller plan
B. Block and Anderson plan
C. corrective instruction
D. Carroll's Model

Short Answer/Essay

18. (4 points) Describe how formative evaluations and summative evaluations are used with a mastery learning approach.

_____

_____

IV. WHAT ARE SOME WAYS OF INDIVIDUALIZING INSTRUCTION?

True or False

19. (1 point) _____ All of the following are examples of individualized instruction EXCEPT

A. peer tutoring
B. programmed instruction
C. cross-age tutoring
D. norm-referenced evaluation

20. (1 point) _____ According to research cited in the text, which type of tutoring situation is most effective?

A. same-age peer tutoring
B. cross-age, same-ability tutoring
C. same-ability peer tutoring
D. cross-age, cross-ability tutoring

126

21. (1 point) _____ All of the following statements about programmed instruction are true
EXCEPT

A. One advantage of programmed instruction is that large skills are broken
down into subskills where students proceed step-by-step through a process.
B. One advantage of programmed instruction is that it effectively increases a
student's level of achievement across all subject areas.
C. One disadvantage of programmed instruction is that its benefits are often
offset by losses in quality of instruction, student motivation, and instructional
time.
D. One disadvantage of programmed instruction is that teachers often spend too
much time on non-teaching tasks.

22. (1 point) _____ Adult tutoring has all of the following features EXCEPT it

A. is one of the most effective instructional strategies known.
B. is expensive.
C. makes use of volunteers.
D. is ineffective with low achievers.

Short Answer/Essay
23. (3 points)   Give three examples of "informal remediation."

_____

_____

_____

24. (3 points)   Give three examples of "informal enrichment."

_____

_____

_____

V.   WHAT EDUCATION PROGRAMS EXIST FOR STUDENTS PLACED AT RISK?

True or False
25. (1 point) _____ Compensatory education is designed to prevent or remediate learning problems
among student who are from low income families or who attend schools in
low income communities.

Short Answer/Essay
26. (3 point)   Explain why the term *at risk* was replaced by the term *placed at risk*.

_____

_____

_____

27. (4 points) _____

Matching

programs designed to overcome problems associated with low socioeconomic status

A. early intervention

B. compensatory

_____ programs that emphasize infant stimulation, parent training, and other services from birth to age five

C. Chapter 1

D. pull out

_____ programs that are federally funded for schools to provide extra educational services

_____ programs in which students are placed in separate classes for remediation

28. (3 points)

Short Answer/Essay

Write a brief description of the Reading Recovery program, early intervention, and Success for All.

_____

_____

_____

SCORING:	POINTS NEEDED FOR MASTERY	POINTS RECEIVED
I. WHAT ARE ELEMENTS OF EFFECTIVE INSTRUCTION?	9	_____
II. HOW ARE STUDENTS GROUPED TO ACCOMMODATE ACHIEVEMENT DIFFERENCES?	9	_____
III. WHAT IS MASTERY LEARNING?	9	_____
IV. WHAT ARE SOME WAYS OF INDIVIDUALIZING INSTRUCTION?	9	_____
V. WHAT EDUCATION PROGRAMS EXIST FOR STUDENTS PLACED AT RISK?	9	_____

FOR YOUR INFORMATION

This section of the study guide includes suggestions for further study of the information you have not yet mastered. You will find information on: 1) typical responses to the SELF-CHECK item(s) from the text; and 2) key concepts, principles, and theories addressed in the text chapter.

I. WHAT ARE ELEMENTS OF EFFECTIVE INSTRUCTION BEYOND A GOOD LESSON?

1. SELF-CHECK ITEM: Draw a diagram or concept map showing the significance of and interrelationship among the following terms: strong incentive, appropriate levels of instruction, high quality of curriculum, high quality of lesson presentation, effective instruction, optimal use of time.

TYPICAL RESPONSE: Draw a concept map.

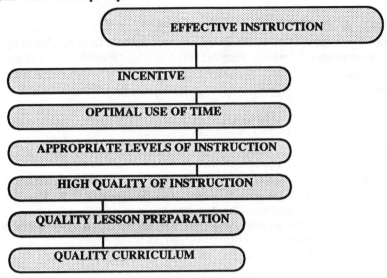

II. HOW ARE STUDENTS GROUPED TO ACCOMMODATE ACHIEVEMENT DIFFERENCES?

1. SELF-CHECK ITEM: Name and define the two broad types of ability grouping. Then give examples of their appropriate use. What is their comparative effectiveness in light of educational research?

TYPICAL RESPONSE: Name, define, and give examples of two ability groupings.

    1. between-class ability grouping: tracking or regrouping into separate classes for particular subjects during part of the school day, such as during pre-algebra or advanced algebra

    2. within-class ability grouping: to place students from a mixed-ability class into an appropriate group

TYPICAL RESPONSE: Evaluate and compare their effectiveness in light of educational research.

Within-class grouping is more effective than between-class grouping because it provides students with a sense of belonging in the class. Between-class grouping is least beneficial for low-track students because: it is often done on the basis of standardized test scores and not on course content, it exposes students to too few positive role models, and, according to the research, teachers of low-track classes are less enthusiastic, less organized, and teach fewer facts and concepts than do teachers of high-track classes.

3. KEY CONCEPTS, PRINCIPLES, AND THEORIES

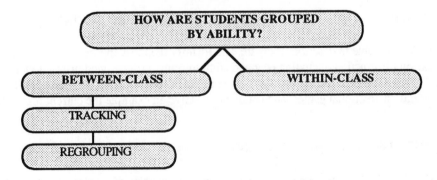

III. WHAT IS MASTERY LEARNING?

1. SELF-CHECK ITEM: Be able to a) define mastery learning; b) explain its underlying philosophy and assumptions; c) describe the different forms it can take; d) describe how the form developed by Block and Anderson works; and e) identify appropriate contexts for using mastery learning. Specifically, be able to explain formative assessment, summative assessment, corrective instruction, and enrichment. Also, relate mastery learning to outcome based education.

TYPICAL RESPONSE: Explain mastery learning.

    a. Mastery learning is a system of instruction that emphasizes the achievement of an instructional objective by allowing time for learning to vary.
    b. Mastery learning is based on the idea that all or almost all students should have learned a particular skill to a preestablished mastery criterion prior to moving on to the next skill.
    c. Mastery learning forms include Bloom, Block and Anderson, and Keller.
    d. The Block and Anderson plan provides corrective instruction during class time for those who do not meet the mastery criterion and enrichment activities for those who do.

e.	1) formative assessment:	test of an objective to determine whether or not additional instruction is needed
	2) summative assessment:	final test of an objective
	3) corrective instruction:	additional assignments or activities designed to re-teach concepts to students who do not meet the mastery criterion
	4. enrichment:	additional assignments or activities designed to broaden or deepen the knowledge of students who meet the mastery criterion

    f. Outcome based education is an approach to instruction that emphasizes clear specification of what students should know and be able to do at the end of a course of study, and then directs time and resources to meeting that goal.

2. KEY CONCEPTS, PRINCIPLES, AND THEORIES

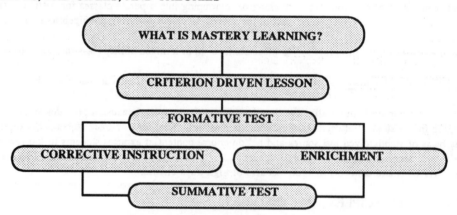

IV. WHAT ARE SOME WAYS OF INDIVIDUALIZING INSTRUCTION?

1. SELF-CHECK ITEM: Be able to describe, compare, and identify the most appropriate uses of the methods of individualizing instruction, including peer and adult tutoring, programmed instruction, remediation and enrichment, and computer based instruction. Give an example of the following computer applications: drill and practice, tutorial, instructional games, and simulations. Give an example the current research on computer-based instruction.

TYPICAL RESPONSE: Describe, compare, and identify uses of methods to individualize instruction.

    1) tutoring: There are several types of tutoring including adult tutoring and peer tutoring. With

	adult tutoring, one-to-one tutoring is most effective. With peer tutoring, cross-age (where the tutor is older than the tutee) is more effective than same-age peer tutoring.
2) programmed instruction:	Programmed instruction materials typically break large skills into smaller skills so that students can work step-by-step. While the idea is feasible, most research has not demonstrated that programmed instruction is effective.
3) informal remediation and enrichment:	This is the most common means of individualizing instruction. Teachers attempt to make informal adjustments during whole class instruction. Extra help is provided for those who need it during seatwork (remediation). Extra activities, such as going to the library or computer room, are provided for those who do not need help (enrichment).
4) computer-assisted instruction:	There are several types of computer-assisted instruction. Drill and practice is a widely used, repetitious format where computers provide independent, self-paced practice drills. Tutorials give students self-paced instruction guided by questions. Computer simulation teaches facts, promotes problem solving, and motivates interest by presenting students with realistic models. Educational games are designed to provide students with problem solving abilities, reinforce skills and knowledge, and motivate interest in learning. Utility programs are general purpose programs such as word processing or text editing.

TYPICAL RESPONSE: Give an example of drill and practice, tutorials, games, and simulations.

1) drill and practice	practicing history facts
2) tutorials	learning a new skill in math
3) games	Where in the World is Carmen Sandiego?
4) simulations	Oregon Trail

2. KEY CONCEPTS, PRINCIPLES, AND THEORIES

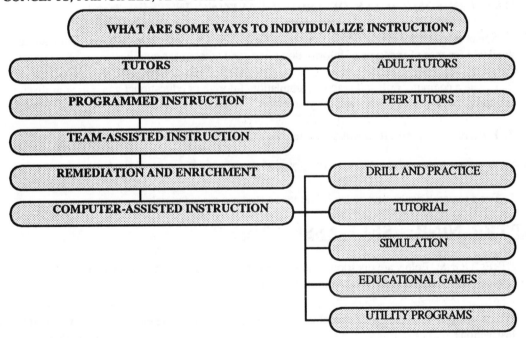

FOR YOUR ENJOYMENT

This section of the study guide includes suggestions for enriching your understanding of a chapter heading you have mastered. You will find information on activities related to the heading and suggestions for research papers, interviews, or presentations.

I. WHAT ARE THE ELEMENTS OF EFFECTIVE INSTRUCTION BEYOND A GOOD LESSON?

1. Observe a classroom teacher and record all the activities that take place in a one hour period, keeping track of the amount of time spent in each activity. Evaluate and report your data in relation to the models of effective teaching presented in this chapter.

2. For a research paper, review the literature on effective teaching.

II. HOW ARE STUDENTS GROUPED TO ACCOMMODATE ACHIEVEMENT DIFFERENCES?

1. Interview a teacher about her or his use of within-class ability grouping. Ask how the groups were formed, what activities the groups encounter, and how the groups are reinforced for appropriate behavior.

2. Describe your ideal teacher for the grade level you plan to teach. Then interview students at that level and ask them to characterize their ideal teacher. How does your description compare with theirs? How do you explain the results?

III. WHAT IS MASTERY LEARNING?

1. Interview a teacher who uses a mastery approach in his or her classroom about its effectiveness.

2. Write objectives, a lesson, and test questions that address one related idea from your discipline.

IV. WHAT ARE SOME WAYS OF INDIVIDUALIZING INSTRUCTION?

1. Select software for instruction in your discipline at the appropriate grade level. Compare the types available for ease of use, type of information given, and assessment qualities.

2. Create a computer drill and practice, simulation, tutorial, or educational game in your discipline which is appropriate for the level of students you intend to teach.

3. For a research paper, review the literature on computer based instruction.

V. WHAT EDUCATION PROGRAMS EXIST FOR STUDENTS PLACED AT RISK?

1. For a research paper, review the literature on students placed at risk.

CHAPTER NINE: SELF-ASSESSMENT

DIRECTIONS: Below are questions related to the main ideas presented in the chapter. Correct answers or typical responses can be found at the end of the study guide.

1.   Which component of the QAIT model is considered to be an alterable element that is necessary for instruction?

    A. quality of instruction
    B. appropriate levels of instruction
    C. incentive
    D. time
    E. all of the above

2. Match the following elements from Carroll's model of instruction with the related description of a hypothetical classroom situation.

_____ aptitude

_____ ability to understand

_____ perseverance

_____ opportunity

_____ quality of instruction

A. Students have the prerequisite skills needed for the tasks that will be taught.

B. The teacher has set aside extra class time to present this lesson.

C. Students are eager to study until the skills are mastered.

D. Students have shown great ability to learn.

E. The lesson is presented in such a way that students learn it as fast as their knowledge and abilities allow.

3. Briefly explain why within-class ability grouping may be preferable to between-class ability grouping.

4. Which of the following statements reflects the major philosophy of mastery learning regarding student differences?

A. allows level of achievement to vary while holding learning constant
B. allow both achievement and learning time to vary as much as possible
C. keeps both level of achievement and learning time constant
D. allows learning time to vary while keeping level of achievement consistent

5. All of the following are central features of mastery learning EXCEPT

A. norm-referenced tests that compare students to each other.
B. formative quizzes that provide feedback on the student's progress while learning.
C. summative quizzes that assess performance at the end of a lesson.
D. corrective instruction that is given when mastery is not achieved.

6. A student receives a computer based lesson about the space program. She proceeds at her own pace, reading the information provided and answering questions that are presented intermittently. On the basis of her responses, either a review or new material is presented in the next segment. This program illustrates which computer based instruction type?

A. tutorial
B. simulation
C. drill and practice

7. Educational programs for students who are placed at risk that prevent or remediate learning problems and target students from poor or disadvantaged backgrounds include all of the following EXCEPT

A. compensatory education.
B. special education.
C. Title I.
D. intervention programs.

8. Refer to the chapter opening scenario. Imagine Mr. Arbuthnot's classroom with vastly improved results. How did he better meet students' needs with techniques such as peer tutoring or ability grouping?

9.   How do traditional classrooms (organized by grades based on student age) impede the use of mastery learning methods?

10.   You want to plan a peer tutoring program in a middle school. On the basis of the research evidence, identify some factors that would improve your chances for a successful program.

PRACTICE TEST ANSWERS

1. D; Whole group, teacher-led activities are not essential elements of effective instruction.

2. B; Achievement equals time needed in relation to time spent.

3. C; aptitude to learn

4. C; incentive

5. B, C, A, D; Appropriate level of instruction requires consideration of students' needs and abilities. Incentive means to give recognition. Quality of instruction includes planning lessons that are interesting, well-organized, and clear. Time refers to recognizing that students will not all complete assignments simultaneously.

6. Student controlled elements include aptitude, ability to understand instruction, and perseverance. Teacher controlled elements include quality of instruction, appropriate levels of instruction, incentive and time.

7. B; Using test scores to place students in different classes is an example of between-class ability grouping.

8. D; A within-class ability group would consist of students who are at different levels of ability working together.

9. A; Between-class ability grouping is advantageous for high-track class members.

10. A; Within-class ability groups can benefit all students.

11. Between class ability groups include college preparatory or general track, math placement, or gifted programs. Within-class ability groups include reading groups, math groups, or study groups.

12. True; Mastery learning is used to adapt instruction to individual needs.

13. D; Students should possess prerequisite skills prior to learning new skills.

14. A; mastery criterion

15. C; an enrichment activity

16. B; corrective instruction

17. A; the Keller plan

18. Formative evaluations are administered during units of instruction. Their purpose is to measure progress, guide the content, and pace the lesson. Summative evaluations follow instruction. Their purpose is to evaluate students' knowledge or skills.

19. D; norm-referenced evaluations

20. D; cross-age, cross-ability tutoring

21. C; It is not true that programmed instruction benefits are offset by losses in quality of instruction, student motivation, and instructional time.

22. D; Same-ability students work together.

23. 1. Providing help to students who need it during seatwork. 2. Work with students who are having problems outside of class (e.g., before school). 3. Have students would together informally.

24. 1. Gifted and talented programs. 2. Assign extra activities to those who finish early. 3. Assign special reports to students who have special interests.

25. True. Compensatory education programs are for students placed at risk.

26. The term *placed at risk* has replaced the term *at risk* because it emphasizes the fact that it is often an inadequate response to a student's needs by school, family, or community.

27. B, A, C, D Early intervention program target infants and toddlers. Compensatory education programs prevent or remediate learning problems for students who are from lower socioeconomic status communities. Chapter 1 programs are federally funded and target low income and disadvantaged students. Pull-out programs place students in separate classes for remediation.

28. Early intervention programs target at risk infants and toddlers to prevent possible later need for remediation. Reading Recovery programs provide one-to-one tutoring from specially trained teachers to first graders who are not reading adequately. Success for All programs provide one-to-one tutoring, family support services, and changes in instruction that might prevent students from falling behind.

10
MOTIVATING STUDENTS TO LEARN

CHAPTER OVERVIEW

The material covered in this chapter focuses on motivation -- the internal processes that activate, guide, and maintain behavior. Some of the theoretical concepts associated with motivation are listed below.

Motivation, depending on the theory, can be a consequence of reinforcement, a measure of human need, a product of dissonance, an attribution of successes and failures, or an expectancy of the probability of success.

Motivation can be enhanced by emphasizing learning goals and empowering attributions.

Motivation to learn can increase when teachers arouse students' interest, maintain their curiosity, use a variety of teaching strategies, state clear expectations, and give frequent and immediate feedback.

Motivation to learn can increase when rewards are contingent, specific, and credible.

CHAPTER OUTLINE

I. WHAT IS MOTIVATION?

II. WHAT ARE SOME THEORIES OF MOTIVATION?
    A. Motivation and Behavioral Learning Theory
    B. Motivation and Human Needs
    C. Motivation and Cognitive Dissonance Theory
    D. Motivation and Personality Theory
    E. Motivation and Attribution Theory
    F. Motivation and Expectancy Theory

III. HOW CAN ACHIEVEMENT MOTIVATION BE ENHANCED?
    A. Motivation and Goal Orientations
    B. Learned Helplessness and Attribution Training
    C. Teacher Expectations and Achievement
    D. Anxiety and Achievement

IV. HOW CAN TEACHERS INCREASE STUDENTS' MOTIVATION TO LEARN?
    A. Intrinsic and Extrinsic Motivation
    B. How Can Teachers Enhance Intrinsic Motivation?
    C. Principles for Providing Incentives to Learn

V. HOW CAN TEACHERS REWARD PERFORMANCE, EFFORT, AND IMPROVEMENT?
    A. Using Praise Effectively
    B. Teaching Students to Praise Themselves
    C. Using Grades as Incentives
    D. Individual Learning Expectations
    E. Incentive Systems Based on Goal Structure

PRACTICE TEST

DIRECTIONS: Each chapter heading from the text listed below is followed by a series of related questions worth a total of ten points. Respond to each question, check your answers with those found at the end of the chapter, then determine your score. Consider nine points per heading to be mastery.

For those headings on which you do not score at least nine points, turn to the FOR YOUR INFORMATION section of the study guide for corrective instruction. For those headings on which you do score at least nine points, turn to the FOR YOUR ENJOYMENT section of the study guide for enrichment activities.

I. WHAT IS MOTIVATION?

True or False

1. (1 point)   _____   Motivation is one of the most important ingredients of effective instruction.

Short Answer/Essay

2. (5 points)   List five factors that can play a role in making students want to learn.

_____

_____

_____

_____

_____

3. (2 points)   Explain how motivation can vary in intensity and direction.

_____

_____

4. (2 points)   Give an example of an activity that promotes intrinsic motivation and an activity that promotes extrinsic motivation.

_____

_____

II. WHAT ARE SOME THEORIES OF MOTIVATION?

True or False

5. (1 point)   _____   For behavioral theorists, motivation is a product of reinforcement.

6. (1 point)   _____   According to Maslow's hierarchy of needs, growth needs must be met before deficiency needs.

7. (1 point)   _____   A psychological theory that deals with behavior, explanations, and excuses used to maintain a positive self-image is expectancy theory.

8. (4 points)

Short Answer/Essay
Attribution theory deals primarily with four explanations for success or failure in achievement situations. List them.

_____

_____

_____

_____

9. (1 point)

According to expectancy theory, motivation is based on what formula?

_____

10. (2 points)

Explain the implications for expectancy theory in the classroom.

_____

III. HOW CAN ACHIEVEMENT MOTIVATION BE ENHANCED?

Multiple Choice

11. (1 point) _____ Which of the following statements best defines achievement motivation?

A. an explanation of motivation that focuses on how people explain the causes for their own successes and failures
B. the generalized tendency to strive for success and to choose goal-oriented success/failure activities
C. motivation created by external factors like rewards and punishments
D. behavior that is directed toward satisfying personal standards of behavior

12. (1 point) _____ Students who take difficult courses and seek challenges are motivationally oriented toward what type of goals?

A. expectancy goals
B. outcome goals
C. performance goals
D. learning goals

Sentence Completion

13. (1 point) _____ According to Atkinson, individuals who are motivated to achieve are called ___.

14. (1 point) _____ An extreme form of the motive to avoid failure is called ___.

Short Answer/Essay

15. (2 points) List two ways in which teachers can make testing situations less stressful.

_____

_____

16. (4 points) List the four general principles associated with helping students who have shown a tendency to accept failure.

_____

_____

_____

_____

IV. HOW CAN TEACHERS INCREASE STUDENTS' MOTIVATION TO LEARN?

17. (1point) _____

Sentence Completion
A type of motivation associated with activities that serve as their own reward is called ___.

18. (1 point) _____
A type of motivation associated with activities that require reinforcers is called ___.

19. (4 points)

Short Answer/Essay
List four strategies teachers can use to promote intrinsic motivation.

_____

_____

20. (4 points) List four strategies teachers can use to promote extrinsic motivation.

_____

_____

V. HOW CAN TEACHERS REWARD PERFORMANCE, EFFORT, AND IMPROVEMENT?

21. (1 point) _____

True or False
Incentive strategies used in the classroom should focus on student ability.

22. (2 points)

Short Answer/Essay
List two ways to reward students' performance.

_____

_____

23. (3 points) List three characteristics of effective praise.

_____

_____

_____

24. (3 points)   List three functions for grades.

_____

_____

_____

25. (1 point)   Define "goal structure."

_____

SCORING	POINTS NEEDED FOR MASTERY	POINTS RECEIVED
I. WHAT IS MOTIVATION?	9	
II. WHAT ARE SOME THEORIES OF MOTIVATION?	9	
III. HOW CAN ACHIEVEMENT MOTIVATION BE ENHANCED?	9	
IV. HOW CAN TEACHERS INCREASE STUDENTS' MOTIVATION TO LEARN?	9	
V. HOW CAN TEACHERS REWARD PERFORMANCE, EFFORT, AND IMPROVEMENT?	9	

FOR YOUR INFORMATION

This section of the study guide includes suggestions for further study of the information you have not yet mastered. You will find information on: 1) typical responses to the SELF-CHECK item(s) from the text; and 2) key concepts, principles, and theories addressed in the text chapter.

I. WHAT IS MOTIVATION?

1. SELF-CHECK ITEM: Write a paragraph stating a definition of motivation, with an extended example illustrating the idea that there are different aims, kinds, intensities, and directions of motivation.

TYPICAL RESPONSE: What is motivation?

Motivation is an internal process that activates, guides, and maintains behavior over time. Individuals are motivated for different reasons, with different intensities, and in different directions. For example, a student may be highly motivated to study for a social studies test in order to get a high grade (extrinsic motivation) and highly motivated to study for a math test because he or she is interested in the subject (intrinsic motivation).

2. KEY CONCEPTS, PRINCIPLES, AND THEORIES.

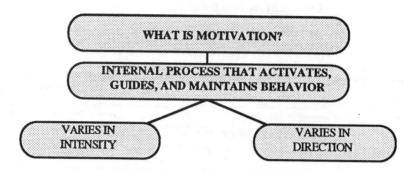

II. WHAT ARE SOME THEORIES OF MOTIVATION?

1. SELF-CHECK ITEM: Organize the information in this section into six schematic representations, one for each general theory about the sources for motivation: behavioral learning theory, human needs theory, cognitive dissonance theory, personality theory, attribution theory, and expectancy theory. For each one, define the underlying concepts, identify any key theorists, experiments, or studies; and briefly describe and illustrate how the model works. Identify features that will enable you to recognize examples of applications and implications of each theory for classroom teachers.

TYPICAL RESPONSE: Organize information into schema.

THEORIES	CONCEPT	EXPERIMENT/ THEORIST	WORKINGS OF MODEL	EDUCATIONAL APPLICATIONS
BEHAVIORAL	motivation is product of reinforcement	Skinner	motivation is determined by personal/situational factors	limited utility
HUMAN NEEDS	motivation is way to satisfy needs	Maslow	deficiency needs must be satisfied before growth needs	meet basic needs first
COGNITIVE DISSONANCE	motivation is satisfying personal standards	Festinger's experiment	conflict causes people to change or justify beliefs	students' reaction to negative feedback
PERSONALITY	motivation is used to describe a drive, need, or desire		strive toward certain types of goals	motivation to achieve
ATTRIBUTION	motivation is attributed to internal and external factors	Weiner	attribute success or failure to ability, effort, task difficulty, or luck	feedback influences students perception of control
EXPECTANCY	M = Ps X Is	Atkinson	maintain moderate levels of probability for success	tasks should be neither too easy nor too difficult

2. KEY CONCEPTS, PRINCIPLES, AND THEORIES

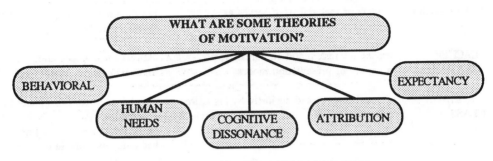

III. HOW CAN ACHIEVEMENT MOTIVATION BE ENHANCED?

1. SELF-CHECK ITEM: Define achievement motivation and contrast the motivational characteristics of students in terms of their approaches to academic success or failure and their goals in attending school. How can attribution training and changes in teacher expectation affect students' motivation and performance?

TYPICAL RESPONSE: Define and discuss achievement motivation.

Achievement motivation can be defined as the generalized tendency to strive for success and to choose goal-oriented success/failure activities. Students can be motivationally oriented toward learning (mastery) goals or oriented toward performance goals. Students striving toward learning goals view the purpose of schooling to be gaining competence. They take challenging courses. Students striving toward performance goals seek to gain positive judgments of their competence. They seek good grades by avoiding challenging courses. Teachers can help students by communicating that success is possible. They can wait for students to respond to questions and can avoid unnecessary achievement distinctions among students.

2. KEY CONCEPTS, PRINCIPLES, AND THEORIES

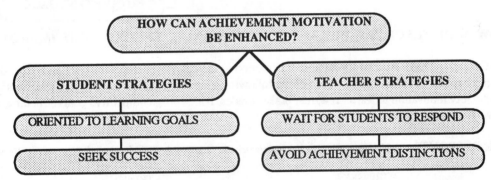

IV. HOW CAN TEACHERS INCREASE STUDENTS' MOTIVATION TO LEARN?

1. SELF-CHECK ITEM: Divide a sheet of paper into two equal columns headed "Intrinsic Motivation" and "Extrinsic Motivation." Then, brainstorm information to enter in each column, including characteristics, examples of motivators, and specific strategies teachers can use to enhance motivation in the classroom. When you have finished, review the section to see if you need to add any important information. Then, reread the chapter opening scenario. Identify each event in Mr. Lewis' lesson in terms of strategies you have listed in your chart.

TYPICAL RESPONSE: Divide a chart into intrinsic motivation and extrinsic motivation and list characteristics of each.

	INTRINSIC	EXTRINSIC
MOTIVATORS	content or material itself serves as motivator	praise, grades, recognition, prizes, special privileges
TEACHER STRATEGIES	arouse interest, maintain curiosity, use a variety of presentation modes	express clear expectations, provide clear, immediate, and frequent feedback
MR. LEWIS' CLASS	aroused interest and curiosity by his attire, role play activity, and presentation style	gave clear directions (secret instructions), provided feedback through formal evaluations on effectiveness of students' presentations, had students work in cooperative groups

2. KEY CONCEPTS, PRINCIPLES, AND THEORIES

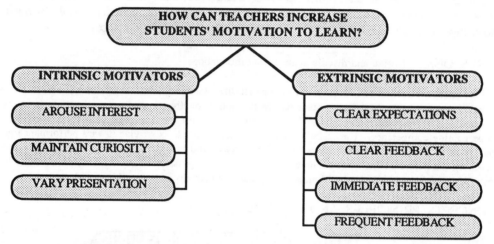

V. HOW CAN TEACHERS REWARD PERFORMANCE, EFFORT, AND IMPROVEMENT?

1. SELF-CHECK ITEM: Add information in this section to the chart comparing intrinsic and extrinsic motivation. Then, briefly explain and illustrate how each of the following strategies could be used appropriately as incentives to enhance students' motivation to learn: rewards, praise, grades, ILE scores, competitive goals structures, and cooperative goal structures.

TYPICAL RESPONSE: Add information to intrinsic/extrinsic chart (objective four).

	INTRINSIC	EXTRINSIC
MOTIVATORS	content or material itself serves as motivator	praise, grades, recognition, prizes, special privilege, ILE scores, competitive goal structure, cooperative goal structure
TEACHER STRATEGIES	arouse interest, maintain curiosity, use a variety of presentation modes	express clear expectations, provide clear, immediate, and frequent feedback
MR. LEWIS' CLASS	aroused interest and curiosity by his attire, role play activity, and presentation style	gave clear directions (secret instructions), provided feedback through formal evaluations on effectiveness of students' presentations, had students work in cooperative groups

TYPICAL RESPONSE: Explain incentive strategies.

rewards:	should be for effort rather than ability
praise:	praise frequently, making sure it is contingent, specific, and credible
grades:	serves three functions: evaluation, feedback, and incentive
ILE scores:	to recognize improvement until students are performing at their peak level
competitive goal structure:	one student's success necessitates another's failure
cooperative goal structure:	recognize efforts of group so that one student's success facilitates another's success

2. KEY CONCEPTS, PRINCIPLES, AND THEORIES

FOR YOUR ENJOYMENT

This section of the study guide includes suggestions for enriching your understanding of a chapter heading you have mastered. You will find information on activities related to the heading and suggestions for research papers, interviews, or presentation; and 3) related references.

I. WHAT IS MOTIVATION?

1. Make a list of activities that motivate you, your classmates, and students who you will teach.

II. WHAT ARE SOME THEORIES OF MOTIVATION?

1. For a research paper, review the literature on theories of motivation.

III. HOW CAN ACHIEVEMENT MOTIVATION BE ENHANCED?

1. Interview students about test anxiety. To what do they attribute their anxiety? Analyze their responses in relationship to attribution theory.

2. For a research paper, review the literature on learned helplessness and text anxiety.

IV. HOW CAN TEACHERS INCREASE STUDENTS' MOTIVATION TO LEARN?

1. Create a lesson that includes strategies for increasing students' motivation.

2. Observe in a classroom for one or two hours. Make a list of intrinsic and extrinsic motivational strategies used by the teacher.

1. Identify rewards you will use in your classroom to improve performance and effort.

CHAPTER TEN: SELF-ASSESSMENT

DIRECTIONS: Below are questions related to the main ideas presented in the chapter. Correct answers or typical responses can be found at the end of the study guide.

1.   The following needs from Maslow's hierarchy are listed in alphabetical order. Sequence them in the correct order of the hierarchy, starting with the most basic.

   A. aesthetic
   B. belongingness and love
   C. need to know and understand
   D. physiological
   E. safety
   F. self-actualization
   G. self-esteem

2.   Match each theory of motivation with the correct descriptive characteristic.

   _____ cognitive dissonance   A. Motivation hinges on whether success is linked to internal or external factors.

   _____ attribution

                                      B. Motivation is triggered by the need to resolve inconsistent perceptions.

   _____ expectancy

                                      C. Motivational levels depend on value and perceived change of success.

3.   A student with an internal locus of control is likely to attribute a high test grade to

   A. the test being easy.
   B. favored treatment from the teacher.
   C. careful studying.
   D. good luck.

4.   Teachers who want their students to try harder regardless of ability level or task difficulty are trying to develop attributions that fall into which category?

   A. internal, stable
   B. internal, unstable
   C. external, stable
   D. external, unstable

5.   A student who tends to choose either very easy or very hard tasks would most likely be

   A. seeking success.
   B. avoiding failure.
   C. risking learned helplessness.
   D. choosing an internal locus of control.

6. Which behavior is characteristic of students who are motivationally oriented toward learning goals?

    A. taking a challenging course
    B. trying to make the honor roll
    C. trying to obtain positive recognition from the teacher
    D. becoming discouraged in the face of obstacles

7. The main idea underlying the Individual Learning Expectations model is

    A. a pass or fail system.
    B. an ungraded evaluation.
    C. grading on the basis of improvement.
    D. grading on the basis of comparison with other students.

8. Match the following goal structures with the correct description of each.

    _____ competitive   A. All succeed or all fail.

    _____ cooperative   B. One person's success or failure has no influence on another.

    _____ individualized   C. Some will succeed and some will fail.

9. Refer to the scenario with Mr. Lewis at the beginning of the chapter. How might the approach be adapted or modified to foster motivation in other subject areas?

10. How would Skinner's explanation of a student's incentive to obtain good grades differ from Maslow's?

11. What is your view on the advantages and disadvantages of being graded on improvement? What arguments would you offer to support a recommendation that such a grading system be used in this course?

PRACTICE TEST ANSWERS

1. True; Motivation is one of the most important components of learning.

2. Students' personality, students' abilities, characteristics of the learning task, incentives for learning, setting teacher behavior

3. Motivation varies in intensity: one student may be more interested in a learning task than another student. Motivation varies in direction: two students can be equally motivated; however, at different tasks.

4. Making a lesson fun, active, and engaging promotes intrinsic motivation. Grades and other rewards, like praise or tokens, promote extrinsic motivation.

5. True; Behavioral theorists argue that there is no need to separate theories of learning from theories of motivation since both are products of reinforcement.

6. False; Deficiency needs are those that are critical to physical and psychological well-being. Growth needs are those that promote understanding, beauty, and relationships.

7. False; A psychological theory that deals with behavior, explanations, and excuses used to maintain a positive self-image is cognitive dissonance theory.

8. Ability, effort, task difficulty, luck

9. motivation = perceived possibility of success x incentive value of success

10. Tasks for students should be neither too difficult nor too easy.

11. B; Achievement motivation is the general desire to be successful and goal-oriented.

12. D; Learning goals-oriented students see the purpose of schooling as gaining competence.

13. Success seekers

14. Learned helplessness

15. Avoid time pressures, begin the test with easy problems, use a simple test format.

16. Accentuate the positive, eliminate the negative, go from familiar to the new, create appropriate problem solving challenges.

17. Intrinsic motivation

18. Extrinsic motivation

19. Arouse interest, maintain curiosity, use a variety of presentation modes, guide learning.

20. Express clear expectations, provide clear feedback, provide immediate feedback, provide frequent feedback.

21. False; Incentive strategies should focus on effort rather than ability.

22. Rewarding directly through praise or indirectly through grades

23. Praise must be contingent upon the task, specific as to what is good, and credible.

24. Evaluation, feedback, incentives

25. Goal structure refers to the degree to which students are in cooperation or competition with one another.

11
CLASSROOM MANAGEMENT

CHAPTER OVERVIEW

The focus of this chapter is on prevention of discipline problems as the most effective means of classroom management. Preventing disruptive behaviors increases instructional time, improves teaching effectiveness, and increases on-task student behaviors. Some of the effective prevention strategies are listed below.

Classroom management strategies that impact the amount of time used for learning include avoiding late starts and early finishes, avoiding interruptions, handling routine procedures smoothly and quickly, anticipating needs, and minimizing time spent on discipline.

Classroom management practices that contribute to effective classroom routines start on the first day of school. Developing class rules and procedures that are presented and applied at the beginning of the school year are important prevention strategies.

Classroom management strategies that advocate the "principle of least intervention" are most effective.

Classroom management strategies that apply behavioral analysis are effective in addressing more serious student misbehaviors.

Classroom management procedures that deal with serious student misbehaviors vary; however, those instructors who are effective managers clearly express and consistently enforce their classroom rules in a manner that students believe is fair.

CHAPTER OUTLINE

I. WHAT IS AN EFFECTIVE LEARNING ENVIRONMENT?

II. WHAT IS THE IMPACT OF TIME ON LEARNING?
    A. Using Allocated Time for Instruction
    B. Using Engaged Time Effectively
    C. Can Time on Task be too High?
    D. Classroom Management in the Student Centered Classroom

II. WHAT PRACTICES CONTRIBUTE TO EFFECTIVE CLASSROOM MANAGEMENT?
    A. Starting Out the Year Right
    B. Setting Classroom Rules

III. WHAT ARE SOME STRATEGIES FOR MANAGING ROUTINE MISBEHAVIOR?
    A. The Principle of Least Intervention
    B. Prevention
    C. Nonverbal Cues
    D. Praising Behavior that is Incompatible with Misbehavior
    E. Praising Other Students
    F. Verbal Reprimands
    G. Repeated Reminders
    H. Applying Consequences

IV. HOW IS APPLIED BEHAVIOR ANALYSIS USED TO MANAGE MORE SERIOUS BEHAVIOR PROBLEMS?
   A. How Student Misbehavior is Maintained
   B. Principles of Applied Behavior Analysis
   C. Applied Behavior Analysis Programs
   D. Ethics of Behavioral Models

V. HOW CAN SERIOUS DISCIPLINE PROBLEMS BE PREVENTED?
   A. Causes of Misbehavior
   B. Enforcing Rules and Practices
   C. Enforcing School Attendance
   D. Accommodating Instruction
   E. Practicing Intervention
   F. Requesting Family Involvement
   G. Judiciously Applying Consequences
   H. Using Peer Mediation

PRACTICE TEST

DIRECTIONS: Each chapter heading listed below is followed by a series of related questions worth a total of ten points. Respond to each question, check your answers with those found at the end of the chapter, then determine your scores. Consider nine points per heading to be mastery.

For those headings on which you do not score at least nine points, turn to the FOR YOUR INFORMATION section for corrective instruction. For those headings on which you do score at least nine points, turn to the FOR YOUR ENJOYMENT section for enrichment activities.

I. WHAT IS AN EFFECTIVE LEARNING ENVIRONMENT?

1. (10 points)

Short Answer/Essay
Create a list of classroom management strategies that provide an effective learning environment.

_____

_____

_____

_____

_____

II. WHAT IS THE IMPACT OF TIME ON LEARNING?

True or False

2. (1 point) _____ Two sources of "lost time" are standardized testing and school assemblies.

3. (1 point) _____ One way to avoid late starts and early finishes is to plan more instruction than you think you will need.

4. (1 point) _____ Minor interruptions do little to change the momentum of a lesson.

5. (4 points)   *Short Answer/Essay*
                 List four ways in which teachers can use engaged time effectively.

                 _____

                 _____

                 _____

                 _____

6. (1 point)   Define "withitness."

                 _____

7. (1 point)   Define "overlapping."

                 _____

8. (1 point)   Explain how teachers can avoid "mock participation."

                 _____

III. WHAT PRACTICES CONTRIBUTE TO EFFECTIVE CLASSROOM MANAGEMENT?

                 True or False
9. (1 point)   _____ Elementary teachers need to be concerned with socializing students to the norms
                               and behaviors accepted in school.

10. (1 point)   _____ Middle and secondary teachers need to be concerned with motivating students
                               toward self-regulated behaviors.

11. (1 point)   _____ Research indicates that the first days of school are critical in establishing
                               classroom order.

                 Short Answer/Essay
12. (3 points)   List the three principles for setting classroom rules.

                 _____

                 _____

                 _____

13. (4 points)   Identify the four principles of room arrangement for minimizing disruptions.

                 _____

                 _____

                 _____

IV. WHAT ARE SOME STRATEGIES FOR MANAGING ROUTINE MISBEHAVIORS?

True or False

14. (1 point)   _____   Teacher behaviors associated with low time on-task were also associated with fewer serious behavior problems.

15. (1 point)   _____   The great majority of behavior problems a teacher addresses are relatively minor.

Sentence Completion

16. (1 point)   _____   The term used to explain that misbehaviors should be corrected using the simplest strategy that will work is ___.

Short Answer/Essay

17. (7 points)   List in order from least disruptive to most disruptive the strategies used to deal with misbehaviors.

_____

_____

_____

_____

_____

_____

_____

V. HOW IS APPLIED BEHAVIOR ANALYSIS USED TO MANAGE MORE SERIOUS BEHAVIOR PROBLEMS?

Multiple Choice

18. (1 point)   _____   All of the following are ways in which student misbehavior is maintained EXCEPT

A. teacher's attention.
B. students' attention.
C. release from boredom.
D. group contingencies.

Order in Sequence

19. (6 points)   _____   When the program is working, reduce the frequency of reinforcement.
_____   If necessary, choose a punisher and criteria for punishment.
_____   Establish a baseline for the target behavior.
_____   Choose a reinforcer and criteria for reinforcement.
_____   Observe behavior during program implementation and compare it to baseline.
_____   Identify the target behavior(s) and reinforcer(s).

20. (3 points)

Matching

_____ program in which a student is rated on
behaviors by one or several teachers; then,
if behavior is appropriate for a specified
amount of time, he or she receives a special
privilege or reward from parents

_____ program in which points or some other form
of reward is given (to be exchanged for
something desired) when appropriate behavior
is exhibited

_____ program in which an entire group is rewarded
on the basis of the behavior of the group members

A. daily report card

B. token reinforcement

C. group contingency

VI. HOW CAN SERIOUS BEHAVIOR PROBLEMS BE PREVENTED?

True or False

21. (1 point) _____ From three to eight times as many boys as girls are estimated to have serious
behavior problems.

22. (1 point) _____ Some students misbehave because they perceive that the rewards for misbehavior
outweigh the rewards for appropriate behavior.

23. (1 point) _____ Consistently expressing the expectation that students conform leads to
misbehavior.

Short Answer/Essay

24. (7 points) List seven ways in which serious discipline problems can be prevented.

_____

_____

_____

_____

_____

_____

_____

FOR YOUR INFORMATION

This section of the study guide includes suggestions for further study of the information you have not yet mastered. You will find information on: 1) typical responses the SELF-CHECK item(s) from the text; and 2) key concepts, principles, and theories addressed in the text chapter.

I. WHAT IS AN EFFECTIVE LEARNING ENVIRONMENT?

1. SELF-CHECK ITEM: What elements contribute to an effective classroom learning environment? Make a list of discipline problems that you might encounter as a teacher. How do you plan to prevent these misbehaviors?

TYPICAL RESPONSE: What elements contribute to an effective classroom learning environment?

Elements include preventing and responding to misbehavior, using class time well, creating an atmosphere that is conducive to interest and inquiry, and permitting the use of activities that engage students' minds and imaginations.

TYPICAL RESPONSE: Make a list of discipline problems that you might encounter. How do you prevent misbehavior?

What is considered a discipline problem may differ from teacher to teacher. However, inappropriate communications, disrespect, and off-task behaviors generally affect the learning environment. Teachers who present interesting, well-organized lessons, who use incentives for learning effectively, who accommodate their instruction to students' level of preparation, and who plan and manage their own time effectively will have few discipline problems to address.

II. WHAT IS THE IMPACT OF TIME ON LEARNING?

1. SELF-CHECK ITEM: Review the scenario at the beginning of the chapter and identify all the ways that time was used in Ms. Cavalho's class. Then, describe the distribution and use of school time and differentiate between allocated time and engaged time. What are four ways that allocated time can be maximized? What are six strategies for increasing students' time on task? Use specific examples to show how a teacher might exhibit withitness and overlapping.

TYPICAL RESPONSE: Discuss various ways time impacts learning.

Ms. Cavalho lost time in her classroom when transitions from activity to activity were rough, as with the ability group reading. Students were asked to return to their desks for materials after they were settled and ready to start the activity, thus a "late start." Ms.Cavalho failed to avoid interruptions when considerable time was spent discussing the cough/sneeze issue.

Allocated time refers to the time during which students have the opportunity to learn. Engaged time is the part of allocated time when students are actually exhibiting on-task behaviors.

There are five ways that allocated time can be maximized. They include: 1) avoiding lost time; 2) avoiding late starts and early finishes; 3) avoiding interruptions; 4) handling routine procedures smoothly and quickly; and 5) minimizing time spent on discipline.

There are six strategies for increasing students' time on-task. They include: 1) teaching engaging lessons; 2) maintaining momentum; 3) maintaining smoothness of instruction; 4) managing transitions; 5) maintaining group focus during lessons; and 6) maintaining group focus during seatwork.

In order to exhibit withitness, teachers need "eyes in the back of their heads." This means that they are aware of what their students are doing at all times. For example, a withit teacher leaning over an individual student's desk to help him or her, and, at the same time, knows that the rest of the class is busy. Overlapping refers to a teacher's ability to be actively engaged in more that one activity at a time. For example, a teacher who is presenting a lecture can, without pause, walk over to two students who are off-task and gain their attention.

2. KEY CONCEPTS, PRINCIPLES, AND THEORIES

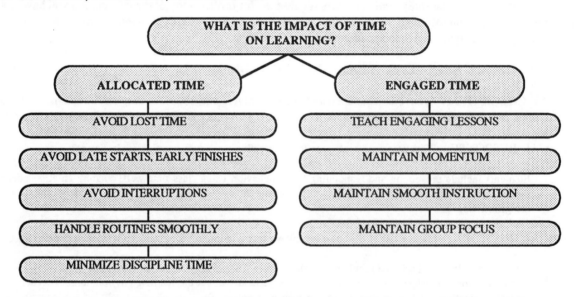

III. WHAT PRACTICES CONTRIBUTE TO EFFECTIVE CLASSROOM MANAGEMENT?

1. SELF-CHECK ITEM: For the grade level you plan to teach, construct a classroom layout and a "to do" list for starting the year in a way that will minimize behavior problems. Annotate your layout and list to identify the principles of problem intervention being applied.

TYPICAL RESPONSE: Construct a classroom and a "to do" list.

To Do:
* keep high-traffic areas free of congestion
* make all students visible to the teacher
* keep frequently used materials and supplies accessible
* arrange room so all students can see presentation

Rules:
* be courteous
* respect property
* be on-task

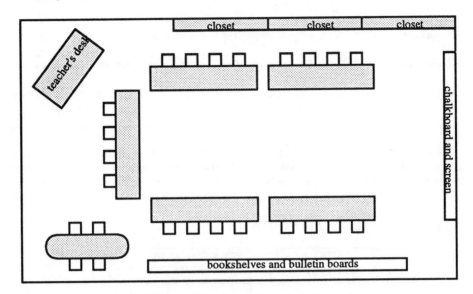

2. KEY CONCEPTS, PRINCIPLES, AND THEORIES

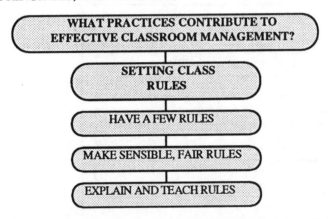

IV. WHAT ARE SOME STRATEGIES FOR MANAGING ROUTINE MISBEHAVIORS?

1. SELF-CHECK ITEM: List the sequence of strategies in the principles of least intervention that are used for managing routine misbehavior. In each case, how does the strategy work? How would you identify examples of these strategies in student-teacher dialogues? Reread the scenario at the beginning of this chapter. How could Ms. Cavalho have managed her students' misbehavior?

TYPICAL RESPONSE: Discuss the principles of least intervention.

SEQUENCE	HOW STRATEGY WORKS
prevention	present interesting lessons, make class rules clear and consistent, keep students busy

157

nonverbal cues	make eye contact, move closer to misbehaving students, light touch on shoulder
praise good behavior	praise students when they are exhibiting appropriate behaviors
praise other students	praise students who are exhibiting appropriate behaviors as a cue to those who are misbehaving
verbal reminder	soft, simple, immediate verbal reprimand
repeated reminder	includes statement of what is expected, given until student complies
applying consequences	examples include sending students out of class, making students stay after school, removing privileges, and calling students' parents

Ms. Cavalho could have prevented many of her problems by being prepared. Students, prior to moving to another area of the classroom, should have been told exactly what they needed to take with them. This would have eliminated the trips back to their desks for materials. A nonverbal cue to the girl who sneezed (e.g., making eye contact and then directing her by pointing to the tissue on the desk) would have solved this problem.

2. KEY CONCEPTS, PRINCIPLES, AND THEORIES

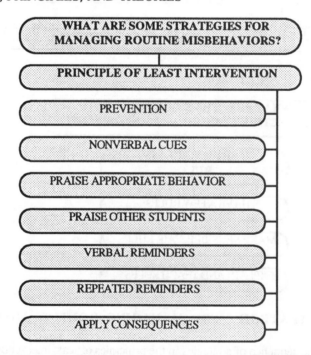

V. HOW IS APPLIED BEHAVIOR ANALYSIS USED TO MANAGE MORE SERIOUS BEHAVIOR PROBLEMS?

1. SELF-CHECK ITEM: Explain how applied behavior analysis is done. Then, describe the appropriate and ethical use of each of the following applications of principles of behavior modification: praise, home-based reinforcement, token reinforcement, punishment, daily report cards, and group contingencies.

TYPICAL RESPONSE: Discuss applied behavior analysis.

There are six steps to setting up and using applied behavior analysis in the classroom: 1) identify target behavior(s) and reinforcer(s); 2) establish a baseline for the target behavior; 3) choose a reinforcer and criteria for reinforcement; 4) if necessary, choose a punisher and criteria for punishment; 5) observe behavior during program implementation and compare it to baseline; and 6) when the program is working, reduce the frequency of reinforcement.

Home-based reinforcement strategies and daily report card programs (a type of home-based reinforcement strategy) service individual students. With home-based programs, teachers give students a daily or weekly report card (contract) to take home and students are instructed to provide special privileges or rewards to students on the basis of these reports.

Token reinforcement and group contingency programs are examples of behavioral analysis applied to whole groups. Token reinforcement uses points or tokens (some sort of symbolic reward) that can be exchanged for desired rewards when appropriate behavior has been exhibited by the class. Group contingency is a reinforcement program in which an entire group is rewarded on the basis of the behavior of each of the group members.

2. KEY CONCEPTS, PRINCIPLES, AND THEORIES

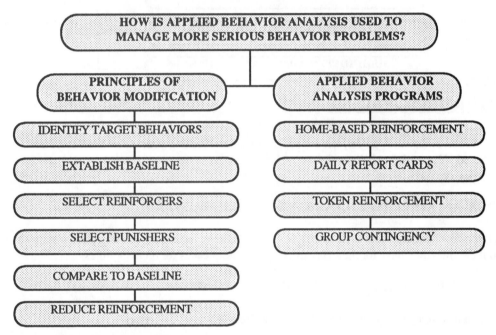

VI. HOW CAN SERIOUS DISCIPLINE PROBLEMS BE PREVENTED?

1. SELF-CHECK ITEM: Evaluate and discuss with classmates the general strategies presented in this section for prevention and intervention against serious school discipline problems. Develop a five-point action plan for best preventing delinquency among your students.

TYPICAL RESPONSE: Develop a five-point plan.

1. Enforce classroom rules and practices consistently and fairly.
2. Accommodate instruction to meet the diverse needs of all learners.
3. Practice prevention first, then intervention.
4. Involve parents.
5. Judiciously apply consequences.

2. KEY CONCEPTS, PRINCIPLES, AND THEORIES

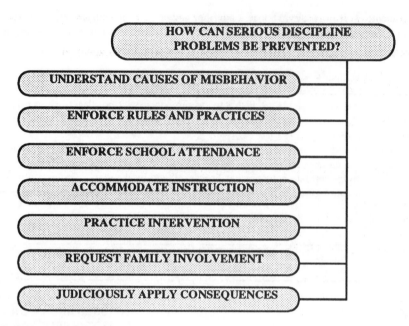

HOW CAN SERIOUS DISCIPLINE
PROBLEMS BE PREVENTED?

UNDERSTAND CAUSES OF MISBEHAVIOR

ENFORCE RULES AND PRACTICES

ENFORCE SCHOOL ATTENDANCE

ACCOMMODATE INSTRUCTION

PRACTICE INTERVENTION

REQUEST FAMILY INVOLVEMENT

JUDICIOUSLY APPLY CONSEQUENCES

FOR YOUR ENJOYMENT

This section of the study guide includes suggestions for enriching your understanding of a chapter heading you have mastered. You will find information on activities related to the objective and suggestions for research papers, interviews, or presentation.

I. WHAT IS AN EFFECTIVE LEARNING ENVIRONMENT?

1. Interview teachers about their strategies for maintaining an effective learning environment. Ask them about the rules they have for their classes and the consequences for breaking rules.

II. WHAT IS THE IMPACT OF TIME ON LEARNING?

1. For a research paper, review the literature on "time on-task" behaviors.

III. WHAT PRACTICES CONTRIBUTE TO EFFECTIVE CLASSROOM MANAGEMENT?

1. Create a list of classroom rules to be discussed with your students during the first day of class.

2. Discuss the advantages and disadvantages of having students make their own rules for the class.

3. For a research project, review the literature on establishing rules during the first days of class.

IV. WHAT ARE SOME STRATEGIES FOR MANAGING ROUTINE MISBEHAVIORS?

1. For a research paper, review the literature on classroom management.

V. HOW IS APPLIED BEHAVIOR ANALYSIS USED TO MANAGE MORE SERIOUS BEHAVIOR PROBLEMS?

1. For a research paper, review the literature on applied behavior analysis.

1. Discuss with other students your concerns about classroom management.

CHAPTER ELEVEN: SELF-ASSESSMENT

DIRECTIONS: Below are questions related to the main ideas presented in the chapter. Correct answers or typical responses can be found at the end of the study guide.

1. According to research, which of the following would be most likely to increase student achievement?

   A. Increasing allocated time by 10 percent above what it is normally.
   B. Increasing engaged time to 100 percent of the allocated classroom time.
   C. Increasing engaged time by 10 percent above what it is normally.
   D. Decreasing allocated time by late starts and early finishes.

2. A teacher begins the social studies lesson by asking, "Cassandra, what are some of the reasons the textbook lists for requiring people to pay taxes?" Which principle recommended by Kounin has the teacher clearly not followed?

   A. accountability
   B. withitness
   C. overlapping
   D. group alerting

3. Match the following terms with the correct definition for each.

   _____ accountability

   _____ group alerting

   _____ withitness

   _____ overlapping

   A. monitoring the behavior of all students and responding when necessary.

   B. using questioning strategies that hold the attention of all students

   C. maintaining the flow of instruction in spite of small interruptions

   D. involving all students in all parts of a lecture or discussion

4. According to the principle of least intervention, in which order should the following management methods be used in dealing with discipline problems?

   _____ repeated reminders
   _____ consequences, such as suspension
   _____ nonverbal cues, such as a head shake
   _____ verbal reminders

5. Match the reinforcement sought by a misbehaving student with the appropriate teacher response. The student is misbehaving to seek

   _____ teacher attention   A. Send the student to a time-out area.

   _____ peer attention   B. Use teaching methods that provide appropriate levels of instruction.

   _____ release from frustration   C. Ignore misbehavior; praise good behavior.

6.   Sequence the following steps of a behavior management program in the order in which they should be used.

        _____ Select and use reinforcers and, if necessary, punishers.
        _____ Establish a baseline for the target behavior.
        _____ Phase out reinforcement.
        _____ Identify the target behavior and its reinforcer(s).

7.   Daily report cards, group contingency programs, home-based reinforcement programs, and individual behavior management programs are all based on

        A. assertive discipline.
        B. delinquency prevention.
        C. behavioral learning theory.
        D. the principle of least intervention.

8.   Refer to the scenario at the beginning of the chapter. What do you think Gloria's good reason was for being late? What would you do if she were late again? Recall what you know about moral development at different age levels. How do you think the class reacted to Gloria's good reason for being late.

9.   In a short essay, discuss ethical considerations in the use of individual and group behavior management programs.

10.   Explain how you would prevent the following misbehaviors: speaking out of turn, teasing another student for giving the incorrect answer, shoving a student on the playground.

PRACTICE TEST ANSWERS

1. Prevent and respond to misbehavior, use class time well, create an atmosphere that is conducive to interest and inquiry, permit the use of activities that engage students' minds and imaginations, present well organized lessons, use incentives for learning effectively, accommodate instruction to students' needs.

2. True; "Lost time" is the result of any activity that substitutes for actual instruction time.

3. True; On time starts to a lesson that continue until the allocated time for completion result from, at least in part, being over-prepared.

4. False; Interruptions -- even minor ones -- directly cut into instruction time and disrupt momentum.

5. Teach engaging lessons, maintain momentum, maintain smoothness of instruction, manage transitions, maintain group focus.

6. "Withit" teachers are aware of students' behaviors at all times. They seem to have eyes in the backs of their heads.

7. Overlapping refers to the teacher's ability to attend to interruptions or behavior problems while continuing with a lesson or other instructional activity.

8. Mock participation results from an overemphasis on engaged time -- to the detriment of learning -- rather than engaging instruction.

9. True; Teachers at the elementary level need to help students understand what school rules exist and what is required of them.

10. True; Teachers of middle and secondary students need to help students become self-regulated in observing rules.

11. True; Evertson and Emmer found that established routines during the first days of school were critical in making classrooms effective learning environments.

12. Class rules should be few in number, they should make sense and appear fair to students, and they should be clearly explained and intentionally taught.

13. Keep high traffic areas free of congestion. Be sure students can be easily seen by the teacher. Keep frequently used teaching materials and student supplies readily available. Be certain students can see instructional presentations and displays.

14. False; Teacher behaviors associated with high time on-task were also associated with fewer serious behavior problems.

15. True; Most classroom behavior problems are minor.

16. Principle of least intervention

17. 1. prevention 2. nonverbal cues 3. praise appropriate behaviors 4. praise other students 5. verbal reminders 6. repeated verbal reminders 7. consequences

18. D; Group contingency is a strategy in which the entire class is rewarded for its members' appropriate behavior.

19. 1. Identify target behaviors and reinforcers. 2. Establish a baseline for the target behavior. 3. Choose a reinforcer and criteria for reinforcement. 4. If necessary, choose a punisher and criteria for punishment. 5. Observe behavior during program implementation and compare it to baseline. 6. When program is working, reduce the frequency of reinforcement.

20. A, B, C; daily report card, token reinforcement, group contingency

21. True; Research shows that boys engage in serious misbehaviors far more often than do girls.

22. True; Students who do not experience success in school see the rewards of behaving to be small.

23. False; Expectations that students will conform to school rules must be consistently expressed.

24. 1. enforcing rules and practices 2. enforcing school attendance 3. accommodating instruction 4. practicing intervention 5. requesting family involvement 6. judiciously applying consequences

12
EXCEPTIONAL LEARNERS

CHAPTER OVERVIEW

This chapter focuses on the idea that schools are responsible for finding ways to meet the needs of each student in a regular classroom setting, to the extent that it is possible. Described below are some exceptionalities that children may have and programs that have been effective in meeting their needs.

Exceptional learners are defined as those students who have mental retardation, learning disabilities, communication disorders, emotional and behavioral disorders, physical impairments, or giftedness.

Exceptional learners have their needs met through the Education For All Handicapped Act and the Americans with Disabilities Act.

Exceptional learners are mainstreamed into the least restrictive environment possible.

CHAPTER OUTLINE

I. WHO ARE EXCEPTIONAL LEARNERS?
    A. Types of Exceptionalities and Number of Students Served
    B. Students with Mental Retardation
    C. Students with Learning Disabilities
    D. Students with Communications Disorders
    E. Students with Emotional and Behavioral Disorders
    F. Students with Sensory, Physical, and Health Impairments
    G. Students who are Gifted and Talented

III. WHAT IS SPECIAL EDUCATION?
    A. Public Law 94-142 and IDEA
    B. An Array of Special Education Services

IV. WHAT IS MAINSTREAMING AND INCLUSION?
    A. Research on Mainstreaming and Inclusion
    B. Adapting Instruction
    C. Teaching Learning Strategies and Megacognitive Awareness
    D. Prevention and Early Intervention
    E. Computers and Students with Disabilities
    F. Buddy System and Peer Tutoring
    G. Social Integration of Students with Disabilities

PRACTICE TEST

DIRECTIONS: Each chapter heading listed below is followed by a series of related questions worth a total of ten points. Respond to each question, check your answers with those found at the end of the chapter, then determine your score. Consider nine points to be mastery.

For those headings on which you do not score at least nine points, turn to the FOR YOUR INFORMATION section for corrective instruction. For those headings on which you do score at least nine points, turn to the FOR YOUR ENJOYMENT section for enrichment activities.

I. WHO ARE EXCEPTIONAL LEARNERS?

Sentence Completion

1. (1 point) _____ The term used to describe students who exhibit one or more characteristics that in some way affect their ability to learn is ___.

2. (1 point) _____ The exceptionality that is characterized by significantly subaverage intellectual functioning -- which limits communication, self-care, social skills, health, or safety -- is ___.

3. (1 point) _____ The exceptionality that is not a single condition, but a wide variety of disabilities stemming from brain or central nervous system dysfunction characterized by difficulties in listening, speaking, reading, writing, reasoning, or computing, is ___.

4. (1 point) _____ The exceptionality that is characterized by problems with speech and language is ___.

5. (1 point) _____ The exceptionality characterized by problems with learning, interpersonal relationship, and controlling feelings and behavior is ___.

6. (1 point) _____ The exceptionality that refers to an inability to see or hear or otherwise receive information through the body's senses is ___.

Short Answer/Essay

7. (2 points) List one type of physical disorder and one type of health disorder.

_____

_____

8. (2 points) Define "giftedness."

_____

_____

II. WHAT IS SPECIAL EDUCATION?

True or False

9. (1 point) _____ Special education refers to any program provided for children with disabilities instead of, or in addition to, the regular classroom program.

Sentence Completion

10. (1 point) _____ The law that prescribes the services that all children with disabilities must receive is ___.

11. (1 point) _____ According to federal law, the term given to the placement status of students with special needs is ___.

12. (1 point) _____ The term that refers to the placement of students who have special needs with their peers who do not have special needs for as much of their educational program as possible is ___.

13. (1 point) _____ A plan that describes a student's educational needs and delineates a special course of action is ___.

Short Answer/Essay

14. (5 points) Complete the following continuum of services provided by school districts.

1. direct or indirect consultation support for the general education teacher _____

2. _____

3. _____

4. _____

5. _____

6. _____

7. student is placed at home or is hospitalized _____

III. WHAT IS MAINSTREAMING AND INCLUSION?

Multiple Choice

15. (1 point) _____ All of the following are advantages of using computers to instruct students with special needs EXCEPT

A. Computers foster individualized instruction.
B. Computers provide immediate feedback.
C. Computers serve as motivators.
D. Computers keep the rate of presentation steady.

16. (1 point) _____ Which of the following statements justifies the use of "buddy systems" or "peer tutoring?"

A. Buddy systems help teachers with instruction and evaluation of achievement.
B. Buddy systems assist teachers with non-instructional needs (e.g., note taking for students with hearing impairments).
C. Peer tutoring is an efficient method of providing instructional assistance that requires very little training.

Short Answer/Essay

17. (1 point) List one advantage of inclusion programs.

18. (1 point)   List one advantage of pull-out programs.

_____

19. (2 point)   Describe the type of expertise that regular education and special education teachers can bring together to solve problems for students with special needs.

_____

_____

20. (4 points)   List four ways that teachers can foster the social integration of students with special needs into the regular classroom.

_____

_____

_____

_____

SCORING	POINTS NEEDED FOR MASTERY	POINTS RECEIVED
I. WHO ARE EXCEPTIONAL LEARNERS?	9	_____
II. WHAT IS SPECIAL EDUCATION?	9	_____
III. WHAT ARE MAINSTREAMING AND INCLUSION?	9	_____

FOR YOUR INFORMATION

This section of the study guide includes suggestions for further study of the material you have not yet mastered. You will find information on: 1) typical responses to the SELF-CHECK item(s) from the text; and 2) key concepts, principles, and theories addressed in the text chapter.

I. WHO ARE EXCEPTIONAL LEARNERS?

1. SELF-CHECK ITEM: Define exceptional learners and distinguish between disability and handicap. Give examples of each and explain why labeling has limitations. Then, define and describe the characteristics of each of the following categories: mental retardation, gifted and talented, physical disability, vision loss, hearing loss, learning disability, emotional/behavior disorder, communication disorder, speech disorder, language disorder, autism, traumatic brain injury.

TYPICAL RESPONSE: Discuss terms, disorders associated with exceptionalities.

The term exceptionality refers to students who are said to exhibit characteristics that somehow affect their ability to learn. A disability is a functional limitation a person has that interferes with his or her physical or cognitive abilities. A handicap is a condition imposed on a person with disabilities by society, the physical environment, or her or his attitude. Labeling can be harmful because it (unintentionally) stigmatizes, dehumanizes, and segregates those individuals being labeled.

Mental retardation refers to substantial limitations in intellectual functioning that affect an individual's ability to communicate, socialize, take care of himself or herself, function academically, or work.

Learning disabilities refer to difficulties in the acquisition and use of listening, speaking, reading, writing, reasoning, or computing. This wide range of conditions is thought to stem from some dysfunction of the brain or central nervous system. Included as a learning disability is attention deficit hyperactivity disorder (ADHD).

Communication disorders refer to problems associated with speech and language. Speech disorders are those associated with the formation and sequencing of sounds and include articulation (or phonological) disorders, such as omissions, distortions, or substitutions of sounds. Language disorders are those associated with the communication of ideas using symbols and include receptive and expressive difficulties.

Emotional disorders refer to problems associated with learning, interpersonal relationships, and controlling feelings and behaviors. Conduct disorders, while under the category of emotional and behavioral disabilities in themselves, are not recognized for special education services.

Sensory impairments refer to the inability to see or hear or otherwise receive information through the body's senses. Visual and hearing impairments are two types of sensory disorders.

Physical disabilities include cerebral palsy, a motor impairment caused by brain damage, and seizure disorders, caused by an abnormal amount of electrical discharge to the brain.

Giftedness refers to children who are identified as possessing demonstrated or potential abilities that give evidence of high performance capabilities in areas such as intellectual, creative, academic, or leadership pursuits.

2. KEY CONCEPTS, PRINCIPLES, AND THEORIES

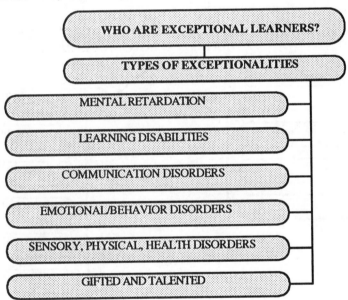

WHO ARE EXCEPTIONAL LEARNERS?

TYPES OF EXCEPTIONALITIES

MENTAL RETARDATION

LEARNING DISABILITIES

COMMUNICATION DISORDERS

EMOTIONAL/BEHAVIOR DISORDERS

SENSORY, PHYSICAL, HEALTH DISORDERS

GIFTED AND TALENTED

II. WHAT IS SPECIAL EDUCATION?

1. SELF-CHECK ITEM: Define special education and explain the main provisions of Public Law 94-142. How have PL 99-457 and PL 101-476 altered the original legislation? Describe the five main kinds of placement services extended to students with special needs and list other special services that are made available. List the minimum information that an Individualized Education Plan must contain. Then, list the steps you would take to prepare an IEP.

TYPICAL RESPONSE: Describe the laws and services provided through special education programs.

Special education refers to any program provided for students with special needs instead of, or in addition to, the regular education program. Public (PL 94-142, the Education for All Handicapped Act) prescribes that services must be given to students with special education needs at the public's expense. Public Law (PL) 99-457 extends the entitlement to free, appropriate programs for children who are infants to five years old. Public Law (PL) 101-476, the Individuals with Disabilities Education Act, requires schools to plan for the transition of adolescents with disabilities into further education or employment starting at age 16.

There are five main kinds of placement extended to students with special needs: 1) regular classroom placement; 2) consultation and itinerant services; 3) resource room placement; 4) special class placement with part time mainstreaming; and 5) self-contained special education. In addition to these services, schools often provide psychologists, speech and language therapists, physical and occupational therapists, social workers and pupil personnel workers, and homebound instruction.

The steps you would take to prepare an Individualized Education Program (IEP) must include the following:
A. initial referral
B. screening and assessment
C. writing the IEP to include:
      1) a statement indicating the child's present level of performance
      2) goals indicating anticipated progress during the year
      3) intermediate (shorter-term) instructional objectives
      4) a statement of the specific special education and related services to be provided as well as the extent to which the student will participate in regular education programs
      5) the projected date for the initiation of services and anticipated duration of services
      6. evaluation criteria and procedures for measuring progress toward goals on at least an annual basis

2. KEY CONCEPTS, PRINCIPLES, AND THEORIES

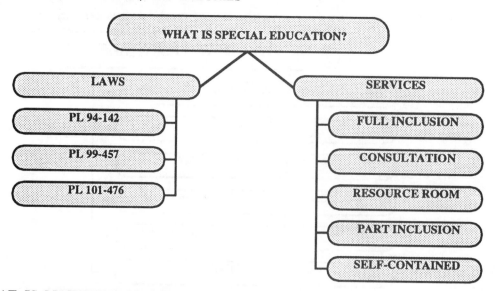

III. WHAT IS MAINSTREAMING?

1. SELF-CHECK ITEM: Define mainstreaming, inclusion, and least restrictive environment. Discuss research findings on the effectiveness of mainstreaming approaches. Describe the most effective strategies for accommodating instruction for classes with mainstreamed students. How do computers, buddy systems, peer tutoring, team consultation, and social integration approaches help students with special needs to succeed? Finally, reinterpret the opening scenario in terms of the information in this section by identifying in greater detail the strategies to which Ms. Wagner called attention.

TYPICAL RESPONSE: Define and discuss the effects of mainstreaming and inclusion.

Mainstreaming is the integration of students with special needs into the general classroom. Inclusion (full inclusion) places students who have disabilities into the general class with support services. Least restrictive environment refers to the placement of students with special needs into educational settings that provide the least restriction.

Mainstreaming requires that students with special needs be placed in the least restrictive environment possible. In general, students excel at a somewhat higher degree when they are placed in the regular education classroom with individual education plans. Highly structured resource room programs have also been found to be effective for those students who need specialized assistance. Some of the most effective programs for working with students who have special needs include cooperative learning groups, computer assisted instruction, buddy systems, peer tutoring, team consultation, and social integration.

Computers provide individualized instruction (e.g., method of delivery, type and frequency of reinforcement, rate of presentation, and level of instruction), give immediate feedback, and hold the attention of students.

Buddy systems help meet the needs of students with disabilities by allowing regular education students to assist with non-instructional tasks, such as providing directions, delivering cues when needed, note taking, and reading.

Peer tutors, who must be carefully trained, can provide assistance by modeling, explaining, and giving positive and corrective feedback. Research shows that both parties involved in the peer tutoring benefit from the experience.

Team consultation brings together the expertise of both the regular education teacher and the special education teacher. The regular education teacher is the expert on how the classroom is organized and operates on a day-to-day basis, the curriculum of the classroom, and what expectations are placed on students for performance. The special educator is the expert on the characteristics of a particular group of disabilities, the special learning and behavioral strengths and deficits of the students who have these disabilities, and techniques for adapting regular classroom instruction.

Social integration requires that the teacher's attitude toward students with special needs be positive and appropriate as he or she serves as a model for the regular education students. Cooperative learning groups also work to socially integrate a classroom.

In the opening scenario, Ms. Wagner calls attention to several concepts presented in the chapter. First, she explains that the school will do everything possible to keep Tommy in a regular education classroom. In the regular classroom, peer tutors and special educator assistance would be provided if necessary. An Individualized Education Plans would be used to help address Tommy's reading or other needs. Parents, Ms. Ross was told, are integral parts of the process of providing appropriate services.

2. KEY CONCEPTS, PRINCIPLES, AND THEORIES

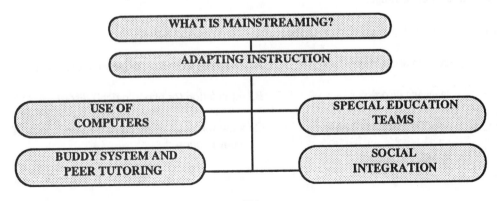

171

FOR YOUR ENJOYMENT

This section of the study guide includes suggestions for enriching your understanding of a chapter heading you have mastered. You will find information on activities related to the heading and suggestions for research papers, interviews, or presentations.

I. WHO ARE EXCEPTIONAL LEARNERS?

1. For a research topic, review the literature on exceptional learners.

II. WHAT IS SPECIAL EDUCATION?

1. Interview a principal, a special education director, and a teacher about the special education services provided to students with special needs.

III. WHAT IS MAINSTREAMING?

1. Conduct a research study about the attitudes of various school personnel regarding the effectiveness of inclusion.

2. Design a lesson, then adapt it to meet the needs of students with various handicapping conditions.

3. For a research topic, review the literature on inclusion.

CHAPTER TWELVE: SELF-ASSESSMENT

DIRECTIONS: Below are questions related to the main ideas presented in the chapter. Correct answers or typical responses can be found at the end of the study guide.

1. Write a short essay explaining and illustrating the differences between a handicap and a disability and the reasons for making distinctions between the two terms.

2. According to the American Association on Mental Retardation, a student with mental retardation who has an IQ between 50 and 75 is

   A. severely retarded.
   B. trainable.
   C. mildly retarded.
   D. within normal range.

3. Match the following conditions with the partial characteristics below.

   _____ emotional disorder   A. reception disorders, expression disorders

   _____ language disorder   B. articulation (or phonological) disorders

   _____ specific learning disability   C. attention deficits, memory disorders, lack of
                                            coordination

   _____ speech disorder

                                       D. anxiety, phobias, aggression, acute shyness

4. List two common options for adapting educational programs to the needs of gifted and talented students.

5. Number the following special education placements in order from the least restrictive (1) to most restrictive (4).

   _____ general education classroom
   _____ part-time mainstreaming
   _____ resource room
   _____ self-contained special education classroom

6. Number the following steps in the IEP process in the order in which they should occur from first (1) to last (4).

   _____ placement
   _____ referral for evaluation
   _____ signed parental approval of the IEP
   _____ testing and assessment

7. What is involved in the effective teaching of mainstreamed students with special needs in a general education classroom?

8. Refer to the chapter opening scenario. Ms. Wagner seems to be providing the best case scenario for a parent with a child who has a learning disability. What is Pleasantville doing that seems so effective?

9. What problems do you anticipate nondisabled students might have in adjusting to students with disabilities in the classroom? How would you troubleshoot these problems?

10. In some areas of the country, minority group students account for one third of the population but two thirds of the enrollment in classes for students with mental disabilities. What are some reasons for this over-representation?

PRACTICE TEST ANSWERS

1. Exceptional learner

2. Mental retardation

3. Learning disabilities

4. Communication disorder

5. Emotional and behavior disorder

6. Sensory disorder

7. Physical disorders include cerebral palsy, spina bifida, spinal cord injury, and muscular dystrophy. Health disorders include AIDS, seizure disorders, diabetes, cystic fibrosis, sickle cell anemia, and bodily damage from chemical addiction, child abuse, or attempted suicide.

8. Giftedness refers to children who are identified as possessing demonstrated or potential abilities that give evidence of high performance capabilities in intellectual, creative, specific academic, or leadership.

9. True; Special education refers to any services or programs provided for children with disabilities instead of or in addition to regular classroom programs.

10. PL 94-142; Education for all Handicapped

11. Least restrictive; The provisions of PL 94-142 state that children with special needs must be assigned to the least restrictive placement appropriate to their needs.

12. Mainstreaming; Mainstreaming places students with special needs with their regular classroom peers for as much of their education program as possible.

13. Individualized Education Program; An IEP describes the student's problem and identifies possible solutions.

14. D; Computers allow for variance in the rate of presentation to meet the needs of the student.

15. Buddy systems involve the teaming of two students, one requiring special services, to work together on non-instructional tasks.

16. Inclusion programs encourage effective partnerships between regular and special educators. Inclusion removes the stigma associated with students who are segregated from those in a regular program.

17. Pull out programs ensure that those educators who work with students with special needs will be trained to do so.

18. The regular classroom teacher is the expert on how the class is organized and operates on a day-to-day basis, the curriculum, and the expectations for performance. The special education teacher is the expert on the types of handicapping conditions a student might have, the strengths and needs involved with the disability, and instruction techniques for adapting curriculum.

19. 1. Model a caring attitude. 2. Use an IEP. 3. Have expectations. 4. Use cooperative learning. 5. Use peer tutors. 6. Provide participation opportunities. 7. Allow for the development of friendships.

13
ASSESSING STUDENT LEARNING

CHAPTER OVERVIEW

The major objective of this chapter is to show the relationships among planning, teaching, and evaluating student achievement. Previous chapters have discussed effective teaching components. This chapter discusses the planning and evaluating of instructional objectives. Listed below is an overview of the important points of the chapter.

Assessing student learning involves the appropriate use of instructional objectives.

Assessing student learning is important because it provides feedback to students, parents, and teachers, serves as evidence of teacher and program accountability, and motivates students' efforts.

Assessing student learning is accomplished through the use of formative or summative evaluations and criterion-referenced or norm-referenced measures.

Assessing student learning is accomplished through the use of well-constructed tests using multiple choice, true-false, completion, matching, short essay, and problem solving items.

Assessing student learning can involve the use of portfolios and other types of performance assessments.

CHAPTER OUTLINE

I. WHAT ARE INSTRUCTIONAL OBJECTIVES AND HOW ARE THEY USED?
    A. Planning Lesson Objectives
    B. Linking Objectives and Assessment
    C. Using Taxonomies of Instructional Objectives
    D. Research on Instructional Objectives

II. WHY IS EVALUATION IMPORTANT?
    A. Evaluation as Feedback
    B. Evaluation as Information
    C. Evaluation as Incentive

III. HOW IS STUDENT LEARNING EVALUATED?
    A. Formative and Summative Evaluations
    B. Norm-Referenced, Criterion-Referenced, and Authentic Evaluations
    C. Authentic Assessments
    D. Matching Evaluation Strategies with Goals

IV. HOW ARE TESTS CONSTRUCTED?
    A. Principles of Achievement Testing
    B. Using a Table of Specifications
    C. Writing Objective Test Items
    D. Writing and Evaluating Essay Tests
    E. Writing and Evaluating Problem Solving Items

V. WHAT IS AUTHENTIC ASSESSMENT?
    A. Portfolio Assessment
    B. Performance Assessment
    C. How Well Do Performance Assessments Work?
    D. Scoring Rubrics for Performance Assessments

PRACTICE TEST

DIRECTIONS: Each chapter heading listed below is followed by a series of related questions worth a total of ten points. Respond to each question, check your answers with those found at the end of the chapter, then determine your score. Consider nine points per heading to be mastery.

For those headings on which you do not scores at least nine points, turn to the FOR YOUR INFORMATION section for corrective instruction. For those headings on which you do score at least nine points, turn to the FOR YOUR ENJOYMENT section for enrichment activities.

I. WHAT ARE INSTRUCTIONAL OBJECTIVES AND HOW ARE THEY USED?

True or False

1. (1 point) _____ Setting out objectives at the beginning of a course or unit of study is an essential step in providing a framework for teaching and evaluating.

2. (1 point) _____ Instructional objectives are statements of what the learner will be like following a unit of instruction.

Multiple Choice

3. (1 point) _____ Which of the following lists represents the parts of a behavioral objective?

    A. performance, behavior, action
    B. cognitive, affective, psychomotor
    C. performance, condition, criteria
    D. affective, condition, action

Matching

4. (3 points) _____ domain that focuses on attitudes such as receiving, responding, and valuing

    A. cognitive

    B. affective

    _____ domain that focuses on physical skill development

    C. psychomotor

    _____ domain that focuses on mental operations

Short Answer/Essay

5. (3 points) List the three steps involved in a task analysis.

_____

_____

_____

6. (1 point)   Describe the process of "backward planning."

_____

II. WHY IS EVALUATION IMPORTANT?

True or False

7. (1 point)   _____ Evaluation refers to all of the means used in schools to formally measure student performance.

Short Answer/Essay

8. (3 points)   Give three examples of ways to evaluate students.

_____

_____

_____

9. (6 points)   Identify six purposes for evaluating students.

_____

_____

_____

III. HOW IS STUDENT LEARNING EVALUATED?

True or False

10. (1 point)   _____ The most effective way to measure objectives is through written, formal evaluations.

Matching

11. (4 points)   _____ form of evaluation that answers the question "How are you doing?"   A. formative evaluation

                              B. summative evaluation

         _____ form of evaluation that focuses on assessing students' mastery of skills, based on some predetermined standard

                              C. norm-referenced evaluation

         _____ form of evaluation that focuses on a student's placement within the group

                              D. criterion-referenced evaluation

         _____ form of evaluation that answers the question "How did you do?"

Short Answer/Essay

12. (2 points)   List two types of alternative assessments.

_____

13. (3 points) List three problems with using grades as incentives.

_____

_____

_____

IV. HOW ARE TESTS CONSTRUCTED?

Sentence Completion

14. (1 point) _____ One way to assure that objectives are being tested is to construct a matrix of the objectives and levels of learning. This is called a(an) ___.

Short Answer/Essay

15. (6 points) List the six principles to follow when constructing achievement tests.

_____

_____

_____

16. (3 points) List three types of items used when writing objective tests.

_____

_____

_____

V. WHAT IS AUTHENTIC ASSESSMENT?

True or False

17. (1 point) _____ Portfolio assessments are a collection of the student's work in an area showing growth, self-reflection, and achievement.

18. (1 point) _____ The research evidence about the reliability of portfolios is promising.

19. (1 point) _____ Assessments of students' abilities to perform tasks, not just the knowledge that is necessary, are called performance assessments.

Short Answer/Essay

20. (3 points) What are three disadvantages to performance assessments?

_____

_____

21. (4 points)   List the steps associated with a performance assessment.

_____

_____

SCORING	POINTS NEEDED FOR MASTERY	POINTS RECEIVED
I. WHAT ARE INSTRUCTIONAL OBJECTIVES AND HOW ARE THEY USED?	9	
II. WHY IS EVALUATION IMPORTANT?	9	
III. HOW IS STUDENT LEARNING EVALUATED?	9	
IV. HOW ARE TESTS CONSTRUCTED?	9	
V. WHAT IS AUTHENTIC ASSESSMENT?	9	

FOR YOUR INFORMATION

This section of the study guide includes suggestions for further study of the information you have not yet mastered. You will find information on: 1) typical responses to the SELF-CHECK item(s) from the text; and 2) key concepts, principles, and theories addressed in the text chapter.

I. WHAT ARE INSTRUCTIONAL OBJECTIVES AND HOW ARE THEY USED?

1. SELF-CHECK ITEM: In a subject area of your choice at a level you plan to teach, attempt the procedures this section describes, and then review the section to see how you can improve on your results. Specifically, practice writing instructional objectives based on Mager's model, perform a task analysis, and use backward planning to sketch out a unit of study. Develop a behavior content matrix with one objective each in the cognitive, affective, and psychomotor domains.

TYPICAL RESPONSE: Write instructional objectives.

> Given a map of the United States, students will label all the state capitals.
> Using the appropriate tools and materials, students will create a piece of art.
> Students will select, read, and interpret a poetry selection.
> Students will calculate the diameters of circles.
> Without error, students will perform each step of cardiopulmonary resuscitation.
> Students will identify the planets of the solar system.
> Students will take a position on a current social issue, using facts to support their beliefs.

TYPICAL RESPONSE: Perform a task analysis and use backward planning.

> Course objective: The students will calculate using addition, subtraction, multiplication, and division.
> Unit objective: The students will calculate using division.
> Lesson objective: The students will calculate double digit numbers with remainders.
>
> identify prerequisite skills: subtraction and multiplication with renaming; division

identify component skills:	estimating, dividing, multiplying, subtracting, checking, bringing down the next digit, and repeating
assemble into final skill:	integrate subskills

TYPICAL RESPONSE: Develop a behavior content matrix.

TYPE OF OBJECTIVE	EXAMPLE
cognitive	Students will discriminate between offensive and defensive plays.
affective	Students will accept responsibly for their roles as part of a team.
psychomotor	Students will perform the physical skills necessary to participate in a game.

2. KEY CONCEPTS, PRINCIPLES, AND THEORIES

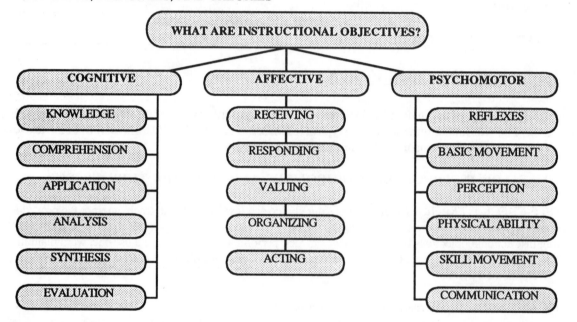

II. WHY IS EVALUATION IMPORTANT?

1. SELF-CHECK ITEM: Identify six primary purposes for evaluating students learning and give examples of each.

TYPICAL RESPONSE: Identify and give examples of evaluation purposes.

PURPOSE	EXAMPLE
feedback to student	specific written assessments of strengths and weaknesses
feedback to teacher	evaluate instructional effectiveness
information to parents	reports of progress (e.g. report cards)
information for selection	placement, tracking (e.g. college prep or vocational)
information for accountability	standardized tests of overall achievement of students
incentive to increase student effort	motivate students with sound, consistent, clear, reliable, frequent, and challenging evaluations

2. KEY CONCEPTS, PRINCIPLES, AND THEORIES

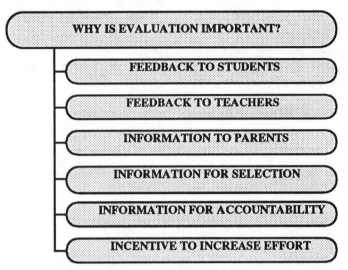

III. HOW IS STUDENT LEARNING EVALUATED?

1. SELF-CHECK ITEM: Construct a four-square matrix comparing formative and summative evaluations on one axis and norm-referenced and criterion-referenced measures on the other axis. In each box, write a brief description of optimal conditions for using each combination.

TYPICAL RESPONSE: Construct a matrix.

	FORMATIVE EVALUATION	SUMMATIVE EVALUATION
NORM-REFERENCED MEASURES	comparison of students to each other to discover strengths and weaknesses for making corrections in instruction	comparison of students to each other to assign grades (on the curve, percentiles) or other final assessments
CRITERION-REFERENCED MEASURES	comparison of students to expectations of identified objectives to discover strengths and weaknesses for making corrections in instruction	comparison of students to expectations of identified objectives to assign grades (points, percentages) or other final assessments

2. KEY CONCEPTS, PRINCIPLES, AND THEORIES

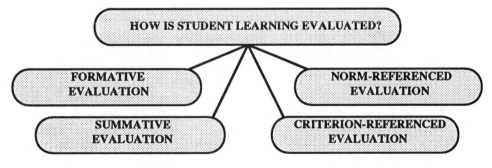

181

IV. HOW ARE TESTS CONSTRUCTED?

1. SELF-CHECK ITEM: Write items for a test on the unit of study you developed in the first SELF-CHECK in this chapter, based on the instructional objectives you developed. Write a variety of test items, including multiple choice, true-false, completion, matching, short essay, and problem solving. After you have written at least one item of each type, review the section to see how you might improve them. List the criteria you will use for evaluating the essay and problem solving items you have written.

TYPICAL RESPONSE: Write test items.

OBJECTIVE	TEST ITEM
Students will name state capitals.	Which of the following cities is the capital of Minnesota? A. Minneapolis B. Indianapolis C. St. Paul D. Bismarck
Students will identify the elementary particles of an atom.	T F Neutrons are negatively charged particles of electricity.
Students will recall famous presidents.	The first president of the United States was _____.

Students will identify composers and their major works.	__ Composer of *Emperor Concerto*. A. Bach
	__ Composer of *1812 Overture*. B. Beethoven
	__ Composer of *New World Symphony*. C. Copland
	                                         D. Dvorak
	                                         E. Tchiakovsky

Students will describe the major causes of air pollution.	List and briefly describe three major causes of air pollution using a five paragraph format.
Students will calculate problems of probability.	If a person is chosen at random from the world population, what is the probability that he or she is from the United States?

TYPICAL RESPONSE: List criteria for evaluating essays and problem solving items.

Essay:
1. Did the student describe three major causes of air pollution?
2. Did the student use a five paragraph format?

Problem
Solving:
1. Did the student successfully use the formula for calculating probability?
2. Did the student arrive at the correct response?

2. KEY CONCEPTS, PRINCIPLES, AND THEORIES

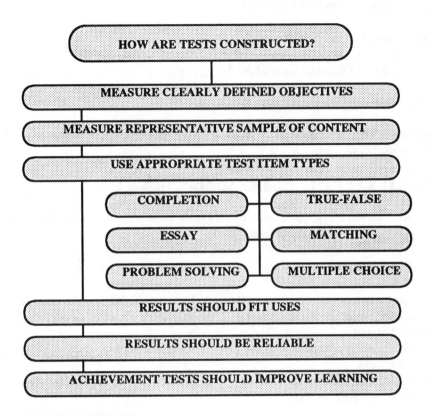

HOW ARE TESTS CONSTRUCTED?

MEASURE CLEARLY DEFINED OBJECTIVES

MEASURE REPRESENTATIVE SAMPLE OF CONTENT

USE APPROPRIATE TEST ITEM TYPES

COMPLETION	TRUE-FALSE
ESSAY	MATCHING
PROBLEM SOLVING	MULTIPLE CHOICE

RESULTS SHOULD FIT USES

RESULTS SHOULD BE RELIABLE

ACHIEVEMENT TESTS SHOULD IMPROVE LEARNING

FOR YOUR ENJOYMENT

This section of the study guide includes suggestions for enriching your understanding of a chapter heading you have mastered. You will find information on activities related to the objective and suggestions for research papers, interviews, or presentations.

I. WHAT ARE INSTRUCTIONAL OBJECTIVES AND HOW ARE THEY USED?

1. Practice writing instructional objectives in the cognitive, affective, and psychomotor domains.

2. Compare Bloom's taxonomy of instructional objectives to Gagne's categories of learning outcomes.

3. For a research topic, review the literature on the advantages of using behavioral objectives and compare it to the literature on their disadvantages.

II. WHY IS EVALUATION IMPORTANT?

1. Interview teachers, administrators, and students on their perceptions of evaluation. Are their beliefs congruent?

III. HOW IS STUDENT LEARNING EVALUATED?

1. Discuss the advantages and disadvantages of norm-referenced measures and criterion-referenced measures with teachers, administrators, and students.

2. For a research topic, review the literature on outcome based education.

IV. HOW ARE TESTS CONSTRUCTED?

    1. Construct a test for your area of study.

V. WHAT IS AUTHENTIC ASSESSMENT?

    1. Create an instrument that can be used to assess learning.

    2. For a research topic, review the literature on authentic assessment, performance based assessment, and alternative assessment.

CHAPTER THIRTEEN: SELF-ASSESSMENT

    DIRECTIONS: Below are questions related to the main ideas presented in the chapter. Correct answers or typical responses can be found at the end of the study guide.

1. Which of the following objectives satisfies (i.e., includes all components) the criteria proposed by Mager?

    A. The student will learn to solve long division problems involving two digit numbers.
    B. Without using a calculator, the student will correctly solve 10 out of 12 division problems involving up to two-digit numbers.
    C. The student will understand how to use a calculator in solving long division problems containing up to two digit numbers.
    D. Using a calculator, the student will demonstrate mastery of long division by solving problems involving up to two-digit numbers.

2. A student is shown a model of a space shuttle and asked to explain what its different components are and how they interact. What type of learning is most clearly being emphasized?

    A. knowledge
    B. evaluation
    C. synthesis
    D. analysis

3. A chart showing how a concept or skill will be taught at different cognitive levels in relation to instructional objectives is

    A. a result of task analysis.
    B. a result of backward planning.
    C. an example of a behavior content matrix.
    D. an example of a table of specifications.

4. Write a short essay on the importance of evaluation with examples of several ways in which evaluations are used.

5. Gronlund's principles of achievement testing make all of the following points EXCEPT

    A. Tests should measure learning objectives that relate to instructional objectives.
    B. Tests should measure a representative sample of the taught content.
    C. Tests should have items of the objective type.
    D. Tests should improve learning.

6.   The purpose of devising a table of specifications in testing is to

A. indicate the types of learning to be assessed for different instructional objectives.
B. indicate the makeup of a test with regard to number of multiple choice items, essay items, and so on.
C. define clear scoring criteria for each essay or open ended question used in a test.
D. compare the students' scores on a stardardized test to those of the national sample.
E. define the normal curve percentile ranks for different grade levels.

7.   Which of the following is recommended in constructing a multiple choice item?

A. Make the stem short.
B. Use none of the above and all of the above.
C. List response and distractors horizontally.
D. Make distractors plausible.

8.   Refer to the chapter opening scenario. Argue that Mr. Sullivan is an effective teacher. Now argue that he is an ineffective teacher. Support your arguments with research and principles that you learned in this chapter.

9.   In a typical portfolio, both subjective and objective measurements are included. Are these equally valid and useful in making educational decisions? Why or why not?

10.   Giving feedback to parents on student performance is part of a teacher's job. What type of grading orientation would be best understood by most parents? How might the choices vary depending on grade level?

PRACTICE TEST ANSWERS

1. True; Objectives guide instruction and evaluation.

2. True; Objectives are statements of learning intents.

3. C; An instructional objective specifically states a performance and may include a condition and the criteria necessary for successfully completing the objective.

4. B, C, A; affective, psychomotor, cognitive

5. Identify prerequisite skills, identify component skills, and plan how component skills will be assembled into the final performance.

6. Backward planning begins with broad objectives for the course as a whole, then unit objectives and lesson objectives are created.

7. True; Evaluation refers to the process of determining student achievement.

8. Quizzes, written examinations, and grades

9. Feedback to students, feedback to teachers, information to parents, information for selection, information for accountability, and incentive to increase effort

10. False; Different objectives have different purposes; therefore, teachers must choose different types of evaluation to measure achievement.

11. A, D, C, B; Formative evaluations monitor student progress during instruction. Criterion-referenced measures are descriptions of performances that are based on clearly defined learning tasks, outcomes, or standards. Norm-referenced measures are descriptions of performances that are determined by a student's relative position in some group. Summative evaluations determine student progress following instruction.

12. Portfolios and performance assessments

13. Grades are given infrequently, grades are too far removed from performance, grades are usually based on comparative standards

14. Table of specifications

15. Tests should: 1) measure clearly defined objectives; 2) measure a representative sample of the learning task; 3) include appropriate items that measure objectives; 4) fit the particular uses that will be made of the results; 5) be reliable and interpreted with caution; and 6) improve learning.

16. True-false, matching, multiple choice, completion, essay, problem solving

17. True; Portfolios are a collection and evaluation of a student's work over an extended period of time.

18. False; The research evidence is largely disappointing.

19. True; Authentic assessments that involve actual demonstration of knowledge or skills are called performance assessments.

20. 1) They are more expensive that traditional tests. 2) Administering and scoring are difficult. 3) It is not clear that they will solve the problems associated with standardized or traditional tests.

21. 1) Identify a valued education outcome. 2) Develop tasks students can perform to support their learning of the outcome. 3) Identify additional desired education outcomes that are supported by the task. 4) Establish criteria and performance levels for evaluating student performances.

14
STANDARDIZED TESTS AND GRADES

CHAPTER OVERVIEW

The purpose of this chapter is to discuss how and why standardized tests are used, and how scores on these tests can be interpreted and combined with other assessment techniques to make important educational decisions such as assigning grades. Information regarding standardized testing and grading is listed below.

Standardized tests are uniform in content, administration, and scoring, and therefore, they allow for the comparison of results across classrooms, schools, and school districts.

Standardized tests measure aptitude, intelligence, and achievement as well as diagnose learning difficulties.

Standardized tests are reported in terms of percentiles, grade equivalents, and standard scores.

Standardized tests must have content, predictive, and construct validity, and they must be reliable.

CHAPTER OUTLINE

I. WHAT ARE STANDARDIZED TESTS AND HOW ARE THEY USED?
    A. Selection and Placement
    B. Diagnosis
    C. Evaluation
    D. School Improvement
    E. Accountability

II. WHAT TYPES OF STANDARDIZED TESTS ARE GIVEN?
    A. Aptitude Tests
    B. Norm-Referenced Achievement Tests
    C. Criterion-Referenced Achievement Tests

III. HOW ARE STANDARDIZED TEST SCORES INTERPRETED?
    A. Percentile Scores
    B. Grade Equivalent Scores
    C. Standard Scores

IV. WHAT ARE SOME ISSUES CONCERNING STANDARDIZED AND CLASSROOM TESTING?
    A. Validity and Reliability
    B. Test Bias

V. HOW ARE GRADES DETERMINED?

    A. Establishing Grade Criteria
    B. Assigning Letter Grades
    C. Performance Grading
    D. Alternative Grading Systems
    E. Assigning Report Card Grades

PRACTICE TEST

DIRECTIONS: Each chapter heading listed below is followed by a series of related questions worth a total of ten points. Respond to each question, check your answers with those found at the end of the chapter, then determine your score. Consider nine points per heading to be mastery.

For those headings on which you do not scores at least nine points, turn to the FOR YOUR INFORMATION section for corrective instruction. For those headings on which you do score at least nine points, turn to the FOR YOUR ENJOYMENT section for enrichment activities.

I. WHAT ARE STANDARDIZED TESTS AND HOW ARE THEY USED?

Short Answer/Essay

1. (10 points) Describe five uses of standardized tests.

_____

_____

_____

_____

_____

II. WHAT TYPES OF STANDARDIZED TESTS ARE GIVEN?

Matching

2. (3 points) _____ test designed to predict the ability of students to learn or perform particular types of tasks

_____ test of a student's knowledge of a particular content area in which her or his scores are compared with others who were tested

_____ test of a student's knowledge of a particular content area in which his or her scores are compared to well specified skill levels

A. aptitude tests

B. norm-referenced achievement tests

C. criterion-referenced achievement tests

Short Answer/Essay

3. (2 points) List two types of aptitude tests.

_____

_____

4. (3 points) List three types of norm-referenced achievement tests.

_____

_____

5. (2 points)   Describe two ways in which criterion-referenced achievement tests differ from norm-referenced achievement tests.

_____

_____

III. HOW ARE STANDARDIZED TEST SCORES INTERPRETED?

Sentence Completion

6. (1 point)   _____   Students' raw scores, which are translated into percentiles, grade equivalents or normal curve equivalents, are called ___.

7. (1 point)   _____   Scores that are reported as the percentage of students in the norming group who scored lower than a particular score are called ___.

8. (1 point)   _____   Scores that are reported as the average scores obtained by students at particular levels of achievement are called ___.

Multiple Choice

9. (1 point)   _____   Which of the following terms refers to the statistical measure of the degree of dispersion in a distribution of scores?

A. standard deviation
B. raw score
C. percentile score
D. mean

10. (1 point)   _____   What type of curve is produced by a frequency graph of a normal distribution?

A. a curve that is skewed left
B. a curve that is skewed right
C. a bell-shaped curve
D. a curve that is depressed at the mean

11. (1 point)   _____   IQ scores are usually presented in which of the following manners?

A. with a mean of 10 and a standard deviation of 1
B. with a mean of 50 and a standard deviation of 5
C. with a mean of 100 and a standard deviation of 15
D. with a mean of 500 and a standard deviation of 50

Short Answer/Essay

12. (2 points)   Explain "stanines" and how they are calculated.

_____

_____

13. (2 points)   Explain normal curve equivalents.

_____

_____

IV. WHAT ARE SOME ISSUES CONCERNING STANDARDIZED AND CLASSROOM TESTING?

True or False

14. (1 point)   _____ The term "validity" refers to the results of a test measuring the type of information purported.

15. (1 point)   _____ The term "reliability" refers to the accuracy of the test results.

Matching

16. (3 points) _____ type of validity evidence that relates a test to other similar measures
                         A. content validity evidence

                _____ type of validity evidence that relates a test to future performance
                         B. predictive validity evidence

                _____ type of validity evidence that relates a test to the objectives of a lesson, unit, or course
                         C. construct validity evidence

Short Answer/Essay

17. (4 points)   List four major criticisms of traditional multiple choice standardized tests.

_____

_____

_____

_____

18. (1 point)   Describe a type of authentic assessment.

_____

V. HOW ARE GRADES DETERMINED?

True or False

19. (1 point)   _____ According to Burton, the reason that primary teachers give grades is to inform students of their progress.

20. (1 point)   _____ According to Burton, the reason that middle and secondary teachers give grades because the school district requires it.

Sentence Completion

21. (1 point)   _____ The term used to represent the grading standards that consist of preestablished percentage scores required for a given grade is ___.

22. (1 point)   _____   The term used to represent the grading standards that rank students from highest to lowest, specifying what percentage of students will receive A's, B's, C's, D's, and F's is ___.

23. (1 point)   _____   The term that refers to establishing a standard of achievement in which all students who successfully meet the standard can review the highest available grade is ___.

24. (1 point)   _____   The term that refers to the number of units students complete in a give amount of time is ___.

Short Answer/Essay
25. (4 points)   List two principles that are important in report card grading.

_____

_____

SCORING	POINTS NEEDED FOR MASTERY	POINTS RECEIVED
I. WHAT ARE STANDARDIZED TESTS AND HOW ARE THEY USED?	9	
II. WHAT TYPES OF STANDARDIZED TESTS ARE GIVEN?	9	
III. HOW ARE STANDARDIZED TESTS INTERPRETED?	9	
IV. WHAT ARE SOME ISSUES CONCERNING STANDARDIZED AND CLASSROOM TESTING?	9	
V. HOW ARE GRADES DETERMINED?	9	

FOR YOUR INFORMATION

This section of the study guide includes suggestions for further study of the material you have not yet mastered. You will find information on: 1) typical responses to the SELF-CHECK item(s) from the text; and 2) key concepts, principles, and theories addressed in the text.

I.   WHAT ARE STANDARDIZED TESTS AND HOW ARE THEY USED?

1. SELF-CHECK ITEM: What is the main difference between standardized and non-standardized tests? How are standardize test results used in student selection, placement, diagnosis, and evaluation? How are results used in education improvement and accountability?

TYPICAL RESPONSE: Discuss standardized test uses.

> Standardized tests are uniform in content, administration, and scoring in order to allow for the comparison of results beyond the confines of a particular classroom or school -- unlike non-standardized tests.

Standardized tests are used in a variety of ways. First, standardized tests are often used to select students for entry or placement in specific programs (e.g., SATs or ACTs) or to decide which students to place in specific academic tracks (e.g., college preparatory or vocational). Standardized tests are also used to diagnosis learning problems or strengths and to determine modes of remediation. Another use of standardized tests is to evaluate the progress of students in particular areas such as math or reading. And, standardized tests can contribute to improving the academic process by holding schools accountable.

2. KEY CONCEPTS, PRINCIPLES, AND THEORIES.

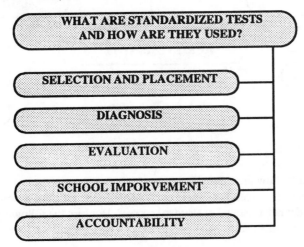

II. WHAT TYPES OF STANDARDIZED TESTS ARE GIVEN?

1. SELF-CHECK ITEM: Compare and contrast aptitude and achievement tests, and give as many examples of each type as you can. How are aptitude and achievement measured? Compare and contrast norm-referenced achievement tests and criterion-referenced achievement tests. Give an example of an optimally appropriate use for each type of test described in this section.

TYPICAL RESPONSE: Compare and contrast aptitude and achievement tests (norm- and criterion-referenced).

Aptitude tests are designed to predict the ability of a student to learn or perform particular types of tasks. The most widely used measures of aptitude are intelligence tests and multifactor aptitude tests. Achievement tests, in contrast, are designed to diagnose student difficulties and to measure formative and summative learning. Common achievement tests include achievement batteries, diagnostic tests, and subject area achievement tests.

Aptitude and achievement tests are measured using either norm-referencing or criterion-referencing. Norm-referenced measures compare a single score to all other scores using percentiles; they are most appropriate when comparisons of this type are needed. Criterion-referenced measures compare a single score, often presented as raw scores, number correct, or percents, to a well-defined set of objectives.

Criterion-referenced and norm-referenced measures differ in a number of ways. Criterion-referenced tests take the form of a survey battery, a diagnostic test, or a single subject test. In contrast to norm-referenced tests that are designed for use by schools with varying curricula, criterion-referenced tests are often constructed around a well-defined set of objectives. Criterion-referenced tests also differ from norm-referenced tests in that measurement often focuses on students' performance with regard to specific objectives rather than on the test as a whole. Finally, criterion-referenced tests differ from other achievement tests in the way they are scored and how the results are interpreted. There is usually a score for each objective.

2. KEY CONCEPTS, PRINCIPLES, AND THEORIES

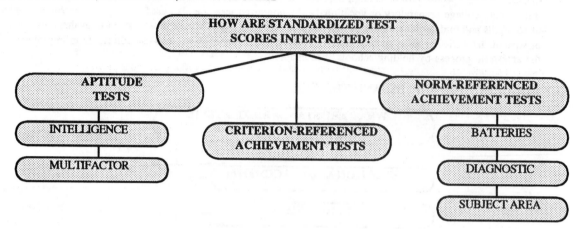

III. HOW ARE STANDARDIZED TEST SCORES INTERPRETED?

1. SELF-CHECK ITEM): Describe how the following kinds of scores are derived from standardized test results and explain how the scores are interpreted: percentiles, grade equivalent scores, standard scores. How are the concepts of normal distribution and standard deviation related to standard scores? How are the following standard scores interpreted: stanines, normal curve equivalents, z-scores? How do IQ scores and SAT scores relate to standard scores?

TYPICAL RESPONSE: Describe percentiles, grade equivalent scores, and standard scores.

Percentiles indicate the percentage of students in the norming group who scored lower than a particular score. For example, students who achieved the median (i.e., 50% scored above and 50% scored below) for the norming group would have a percentile rank of 50 because their scores exceeded those of 50 percent of the students normed in the group.

Grade equivalent scores relate students' scores to the average score obtained by students at a particular grade level. In theory, the score of 5.5 would represent five years, five months; however, grade equivalent scores should be interpreted cautiously. For example, a fifth grade student who scores 7.5 on a measure of math ability is by by no means ready for seventh grade math.

Standard scores describe test results according to their place on the normal (bell-shaped) curve. A normal curve describes a distribution of scores in which most fall near the mean, with a smaller number of scores moving away from the mean. One important concept related to normal distribution is the standard deviation, a measure of the dispersion of scores. The standard deviation is the average amount that scores differ, or spread out, from the mean.

TYPICAL RESPONSE: Discuss stanines, normal curve equivalents, and z-scores.

Stanines are a type of standard score having a mean of five and a standard deviation of two. Each stanine represents .5 standard deviations. Stanine scores are reported as whole numbers; so, a person who earned a stanine of seven scored one standard deviation above the mean (range = .75 SD - 1.25 SD).

Normal curve equivalents (NCE) are another form of standard scores. A normal curve equivalent can range from one to 99, with a mean of 50 and a standard deviation of approximately 21. Normal curve equivalent scores are similar to percentiles except that intervals between NCE scores are equal.

Z-scores, another standard score, are seldomly used as a means of reporting standardized test results. The z-score sets the mean of a distribution at zero and the standard deviation at one.

194

TYPICAL RESPONSE: Relate IQ scores and SAT scores to standard scores.

Scores on standardized tests are often reported in terms of how far they lie from the mean as measured by standard deviation units. IQ scores are normed so that there is a mean of 110 and a standard deviation of 15. About 68.2 percent of all IQ scores fall between 85 (- 1 SD) and 115 (+ 1 SD). SAT scores are also normed according to standard deviations: the mean set at 500 with a standard deviation of 100. Thus, 68.2 percent of the scores fall between 400 (- 1 SD) and 600 (+ 1 SD).

2. KEY CONCEPTS, PRINCIPLES, AND THEORIES

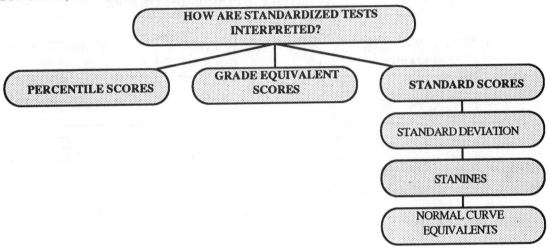

IV. WHAT ARE SOME ISSUES CONCERNING STANDARDIZED AND CLASSROOM TESTS?

1. **SELF-CHECK ITEM:** Use all of the following terms in a discussion or essay about issues in standardized and classroom testing. Include one or more concrete examples of: validity, reliability, test bias, authentic assessment.

TYPICAL RESPONSE: Write an essay about standardized testing issues.

Issues surrounding standardized testing are strongly debated by educators. While they are intended to yield valid and reliable results, several drawbacks exist. One is that they give false information about the status of learning in the nation's schools. The "Lake Wobegon Effect" (note: Lake Wobegon is a fictitious town where "all the men are strong, the women good looking, and the children above average.") demonstrates this. In theory, 50 percent of standardized test scores should fall below the mean and 50 percent should be above. This is not true for several reasons. First, schools, under pressure from the public to produce above average scores, "teach to the test." Also, administrators have been known to "select" high achieving students to take some tests such as the pre-SAT so that overall scores are high. While highly unethical, this procedure makes the school look good; however, some students who could use the practice on the pre-SAT are not given the opportunity to take the test (see *Minnesota Monthly* "Testing: The risky game we play with our children's education" Aug. 1990).

Another debated issue regarding standardized testing is that the test is unfair (or biased against) some kinds of students such as people of color, those with limited proficiency in English, females, and students from low income families. Institutions that create standardized aptitude and achievement tests argue that their instruments are valid measures of basic skills, aptitude, or ability. If the test is not the problem, then either the group (e.g., females) possesses truly inferior skills, aptitude, or ability or has received an inferior education.

Two other problems exist with standardized testing. First, they tend to corrupt the processes of teaching and learning, often reducing teaching to mere preparation for testing. Second, standardized tests focus time, energy and attention on the simpler skills that are easily tested and away from higher-order thinking skills and creative endeavors.

Critics of standardized testing have proposed that schools use assessments that are tied to real applications of learning skills. Alternative or authentic assessment systems such as performance tests and portfolios (samples of students' compositions, projects, or other higher-order thinking activities), serve as evidence of progress. Perhaps the best solution to the controversy over standardized testing is variety. A combination of systematic, objective standardized tests and authentic assessment systems will best reveal how a student is progressing.

2. KEY CONCEPTS, PRINCIPLES, AND THEORIES

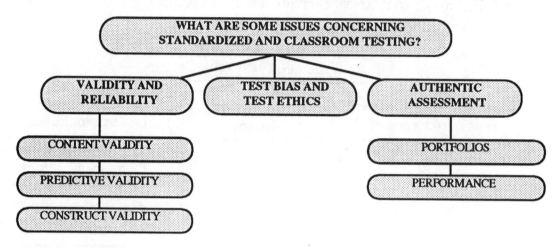

V. HOW ARE GRADES DETERMINED?

1. SELF-CHECK ITEM: Describe the grading system you will likely or preferably use at the level you plan to teach. Briefly outline the advantages and drawbacks of no grades, letter grades, absolute grading standards, grading on the curve, contract grading, mastery grading, and continuous progress grading.

TYPICAL RESPONSE: Outline advantages and disadvantages of various grading systems.

TYPE OF GRADING	ADVANTAGES	DISADVANTAGES
no grades	non-threatening	students perform better under graded systems
letter grades	set by individual teachers set by school administration	teachers can use extremes; either too easy or too difficult
absolute grading standards	criteria for achievement set prior to instruction	students' scores dependent upon difficulty of outcome
relative grading standards	place students' scores in relation to others in group	grades are not representative of achievement in schools using tracking; creates competition among students; artificial boundaries
mastery grading	grades are temporary; allows for correction	progress in relationship to group is eliminated
continuous progress grading	measure of skill progression	progress in relationship to group is eliminated

2. KEY CONCEPTS, PRINCIPLES, AND THEORIES

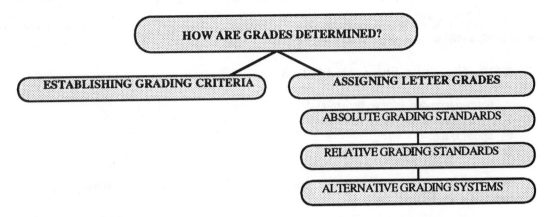

FOR YOUR ENJOYMENT

This section of the study guide includes suggestions for enriching your understanding of a chapter heading you have mastered. You will find information on activities related to the headings and suggestions for research papers, interviews, or presentations.

I. WHAT ARE STANDARDIZED TESTS AND HOW ARE THEY USED?

1. Interview a special education teacher or school psychologist about the types of standardized tests used to assess student performance. Ask how the results are used.

2. Discuss the ethics of holding schools accountable for achievement as determined by standardized test results. Include in your discussion ways that administrators and teachers can raise overall test scores without raising overall achievement.

II. WHAT TYPES OF STANDARDIZED TESTS ARE GIVEN?

1. For a research topic, review the literature on standardized testing.

III. HOW ARE STANDARDIZED TEST SCORES INTERPRETED?

1. Interview a special education teacher or school psychologist about the interpretation of standardized tests. How do they report grades to teachers, administrators, parents, and students?

IV. WHAT ARE SOME ISSUES CONCERNING STANDARDIZED AND CLASSROOM TESTING?

1. Discuss issues related to standardized testing and bias.

2. Discuss issues related to authentic assessment.

V. HOW ARE GRADES DETERMINED?

1. Discuss the advantages and disadvantages to: 1) grading on effort; 2) grading on attendance; 3) grading on improvement; and 4) grading on participation.

CHAPTER FOURTEEN: SELF-ASSESSMENT

DIRECTIONS: Below are questions related to the main ideas presented in the chapter. Correct answers or typical responses can be found at the end of the study guide.

1.   Which of the following types of standardized tests is designed to predict future performance?

   A. norm-referenced achievement test
   B. criterion-referenced achievement test
   C. aptitude test
   D. diagnostic test

2.   Which of the following score reports would apply to a sixth grade student who has scored at the national mean on a standardized test?

   A. %ile = 40, stanine 9, z = 0
   B. NCE = 50, z = 0, %ile = 50
   C. GE = 7.2, stanine = 5, NCE = 100
   D. z = 3, NCE = 60, %ile = 50

3.   Both the first period and fifth period classes averaged 75 on the math final, but student scores in the first class were much more spread out. The first period class, therefore, has a larger

   A. mean.
   B. median.
   C. standard deviation.
   D. normal curve equivalent.

4.   A seventh grader earns a grade equivalent of 9.4 on a standardized exam. Which of the following can be assumed?

   A. She is ready to tackle ninth grade work.
   B. The standardized exam is too easy and needs to be renormed.
   C. She has scored as well on the test as the average ninth grader would.
   D. No assumptions can be made from the one score.

5.   When students take a certain aptitude test twice, they score about the same both times. This implies that the test results have high

   A. predictive validity.
   B. content validity.
   C. construct validity.
   D. reliability.

6.   IQ is measured today on the basis of

   A. Binet's ratio method.
   B. a formula involving chronological age and mental age.
   C. a mean of 100 and a standard deviation of 15.
   D. an average of scores on intelligence tests.

7.   Tests that contain cultural or gender bias lack

    A. validity.
    B. authenticity.
    C. reliability.
    D. accountability.

8.   How can a test be valid without being reliable? Can a test be reliable without being valid?

9.   Refer to the chapter opening scenario. Consider changing the facts of the case. For instance, what if the teacher could not explain the scores? What if Mr. or Mrs. McKay became upset with Ms. Tranh's explanations of their daughter's scores? What if Anita were weaker in math and stronger in writing? Write down your suggestions for handling these situations.

10.   What are the incentives and disincentives of: 1) being graded on the curve; 2) receiving cooperative group grades; or 3) having to get 90 percent for an A?

11.   How would you interpret the academic skills and grade placement of a student who had a stanine score of five on a standardized achievement test?

PRACTICE TEST ANSWERS

1. Selection and placement, diagnosis, evaluation, improvement, and accountability

2. A, B, C; aptitude test, norm-referenced achievement test, criterion referenced achievement test

3. Intelligence tests and multifactor aptitude tests

4. Achievement batteries, diagnostic tests, and subject area achievement tests

5. Criterion referenced achievement tests differ from norm-referenced achievement tests in that they are constructed around well-defined objectives, measured by assessing the number of objectives or "skills" met, and use a cutoff score.

6. Derived scores

7. Percentile scores

8. Grade equivalent scores

9. A; standard deviation

10. C; a bell-shaped curve

11. C; with a mean of 100 and a standard deviation of 15

12. Stanine scores are standard scores that have a mean of five and a standard deviation of two. Each stanine is reported as a whole number and represents .5 standard deviations.

13. Normal curve equivalents can range from one to 99, with a mean of 50 and a standard deviation of approximately 21. NCE scores are like percentiles except that the intervals between the scores are equal.

14. True; Valid test results are a measure of the student's knowledge of some content area.

15. True; Reliable results are consistently accurate.

16. C, B, A; construct validity evidence, predictive validity evidence, content validity evidence

17. Give false information about school's status; are unfair to some groups of students; corrupt process of teaching and learning; attend to simple, easily tested skills

18. Portfolios or performance assessments

19. False; Primary teachers give grades because it is school policy.

20. False; Middle and secondary teachers give grades to inform students.

21. Absolute

22. Relative

23. Mastery grading

24. Continuous progress grading

25. Grades should never be a surprise to students and grades should be private.

SELF-ASSESSMENT ANSWERS   Chapter 1

1. Effective teaching requires critical thinking. It is important for teachers to be able to problem-solve and translate information from educational psychology into sound classroom practices.

2. b. Principles explain relationships between factors, such as the effects of alternative grading systems on student motivation

3. a. In a laboratory experiment controls are put into place that provide the researcher with repeatable prediction of outcomes. Internal validity is the degree to which an experiment's results can be attributed to the treatment in question, not to other factors.

4. d, a, e, c. Randomized field experiment is conducted under realistic conditions in which individuals are assigned by chance to receive different practical treatments or programs. Descriptive research represents a study aimed at identifying and gathering detailed information about something of interest. Laboratory experiment is a process whereby conditions are highly controlled. Correlational study is a research process that looks into relationships between variables as they naturally occur.

5. b. Negative correlations demonstrate a relationship in which high scores on one variable correspond to low scores on another.

6. b. Laboratory experiments by nature offer the greatest internal validity due to conditions being highly controlled.

7. d. By the very definition of negative correlations it is established that high scores on one variable correspond to low scores on another.

8. A good research design might involve both observation and a series of single-case experiments; this would test the effects of random calling on student attention, and test the effects of both random calling and calling in order on student achievement. Similar research suggests Mr. Traub is right on the first assumption, but not necessarily on the second. Random calling seems to increase both attention and anxiety, but the predictability of being called in order may help younger students and poor readers to practice their reading skills more, and thus, show higher achievement. Common sense, therefore, is not enough.

9. Whether the subject is writing, reading, science, social studies, or special education, theories of educational psychology are useful. Knowledge of how individuals of all ages develop and learn are major components of the discipline. In addition, theories of educating psychology help teachers to understand what motivates students, why adapting instruction to meet individual needs is important, and how to assess student learning.

SELF-ASSESSMENT ANSWERS   Chapter 2

1. b. According to Piaget, concrete operations is the stage when students are moving from egocentric thought to decentered or objective thought. Decentered thought allows children to see that others can have different perceptions than they do.

2. c. Vygotsky's proposed that cognitive development is strongly linked to input from others. His work is based on two key ideas. First, he proposed that intellectual development can be understood only in terms of the historical and cultural contexts children experience. Second, he believed that development depends on the sign systems that individuals grow up with. Sign systems refer to symbols that cultures create to help people think, communicate, and solve problems, for example, a culture's language, writing system, or counting system.

3. a. During stage IV of Erikson's psychosocial development the young adult is ready to form a new relationship of trust and intimacy with another individual. The young adult who does not seek out such intimacy or whose repeated tries fail may retreat into isolation.

4. d. Assimilation is the process whereby the individual interprets new experiences in relation to existing schemes. In the correct response the child attempts to apply the same technique to a somewhat similar, yet different situation.

5. c. Gelman found that young children could solve the conservation problem involving the number of blocks in a row when the task was presented in a simpler way with simpler language. Boden found that the same formal operational task produced passing rates form 19 to 98 percent, depending on the complexities of the instructions.

6. a, b, c, d. <u>Sensorimotor stage</u> is the stage during which infants learn about their surroundings by using their senses and motor skills. Learning occurs largely through trial and error. <u>Preoperational stage</u> is that stage at which children learn mentally to represent things. <u>Concrete operational stage</u> is that stage at which children develop skills of logical reasoning and conservation but can use these skills only in dealing with familiar situations. <u>Formal operational thought</u> deals abstractly with hypothetical situations and reason.

7. a, c, b. The <u>preconventional level of morality</u> is the stage in which individuals make moral judgments in their own interests. The <u>conventional level of morality</u> is the stage whereby individuals make moral judgments in consideration of others. The <u>postconventional level of morality</u> is the stage in which individuals make moral judgments in relation to abstract principles.

8. Mr. Jones worked with first graders who were in Piaget's preoperational stage of development. If his students were adolescents or adults, they would have no difficulty raising their right hands before speaking.   This is because they can mentally reverse operations; they understand that Mr. Jones is standing in an about-fact direction, for which they compensate. Ms. Lewis worked with fourth graders who did not understand that there may be exceptions to rules.   They are in Piaget's heteronomous morality and Kohlberg's preconventional stage.   Adolescents and adults, because they can consider intent and circumstances, understand that rules are not always absolute. Ms. Quintera worked with eighth-graders who are, according to Erikson, breaking away from authority figures and connecting with peers.   Young children would appreciate Ms. Quntera's actions.

9. There is a difference between a student's independent reading level, which represents the higher level of Vygotsky's zone of proximal development, and his or her instructional reading level, which represents the lower level. The first describes what a student can do independently and the second describes what she or he can do when assisted by an adult or a more competent peer.

10. Hoffman's theory of moral development takes into account the role of motivation and parental disciplinary practices. He argues that empathic distress -- experiencing the suffering of others -- is a powerful motivator in moral reasoning.

SELF-ASSESSMENT ANSWERS   Chapter 3

1. b. By the end of the preschool years, children can use and understand an almost infinite number of sentences, can hold conversations, and know about written language.

2. a. Psychologists generally agree that play is an important part of kindergarten, needs to be more emphasized, and contributes to cognitive training.

3. b. A main driving force behind participation in compensatory preschool programs is that it increases disadvantaged children's readiness skills for kindergarten and first grade.

4. c. Preoperational thought is that stage at which children learn mentally to represent things. This occurs during the ages of 2 and 7.

5. a. According to Erikson, identity foreclosure is an individual's premature establishment of an identity based on parental choices rather than their own.

6. c, b, a, c, a, a, b. Verbal language, prosocial behavior, and sociodramatic play occur during early childhood; friendships, and conflict management first occur during middle childhood and preadolescence; intimacy and identity diffusion occurs during adolescence.

7. b. Hoffman and Saltzstein (1967) found that parents tend to use three approaches in disciplining their children: 1) Power assertion; 2) Love withdrawal; 3) Induction.

8. Key influences on early elementary students include parents and teachers, from whom they seek approval; however, to a lesser extent than during the preschool years. Peers are beginning to play a major role, beginning with the forming of same-sex friendships. This sharing with others helps early elementary students to sort out and form their own attitudes and values. Key influences on middle level youth include same- and opposite-sex relationships. While there is less need for approval from authority figures (parents or teachers), approval from friends is paramount. Jake's self-concept may be tied to his commitment to help others. Billy's self-concept may be tied to his relationships with an older person.

9. Child development has important implications for classroom instruction at each grade level.

I. Early childhood classroom instruction

    A. Cognitive and language development

        1. Language acquisition and development

        2. Reading

        3. Writing

    B. Socioemotional development

        1. Peer relationships

    C. Instruction examples

        1. Encourage involvement with print

        2. Encourage group work and play

II. Middle childhood and preadolescence classroom instruction

    A. Cognitive development

        1. Concrete thinking

    B. Socioemotional development

        1. Growing importance of peers

C. Instruction examples

    1. Provide experiences that are grounded in the concrete and the familiar

    2. Encourage dialogues that explore values, attitudes, peer acceptance

III. Adolescence classroom instruction

  A. Cognitive development

    1. Abstract thinking

  B. Socioemotional development

    1. Opposite-sex relationships

    2. Identity development

  C. Instruction examples

    1. Provide opportunities that call for hypothetical-deductive thought

    2. Encourage adolescents to explore roles

    3. Discuss health peer relationships

SELF-ASSESSMENT ANSWERS   Chapter 4

1. Multicultural education is not a single program, but a philosophy. Modifications in the curriculum, adaptations of instruction, and changes in the communication of attitudes and expectations in the area of socioeconomic status, race, ethnicity, religion, culture, language, gender, intelligence, and learning styles all contribute to the celebrations of diversity.

2. b. Socioeconomic status is defined in terms of an individual's income, occupation, education and prestige in society. Although it is true that Hispanic and African American families are lower in social class on the average than are white families, there is substantial overlap. Definitions of social class are based on such factors as income, occupation, and education, never on race or ethnicity.

3. d. Middle-class parents are likely to expect and demand high achievement from their children; lower-class parents are more likely to demand good behavior and obedience.

4. An example of multicultural education applied to the curriculum might be the teaching of the westward expansion in America from an indigenous person's point of view. An example of multicultural education applied to daily activities in the classroom and school might include a celebration of a non-dominant group's holiday. An example of multicultural education applied to a teacher's assessment might include questions that are culturally fair and gender neutral.

5. a. The socioeconomic status of various racial and ethnic groups and the groups' scores on standardized tests appear to be positively correlated.

6. a. Bilingual programs have been shown to actually enhance performance in the native language or English. Canadian studies have found bilingualism to increase achievement in areas other than the language studied.

7. c. Feingold has argued that males are more variable than females in quantitative reasoning, which means that there are more very high-achieving males and more very low-achieving males than there are females in either category.

8. a. Intelligence refers to a general aptitude for learning or an ability to acquire and use knowledge or skills. Intelligence quotient, or IQ, refers to an assigned score reflecting the degree to which one performs on an intelligence test. Multiple intelligences refers to the notion that there are seven separate types of intelligence.
   b. Learning preferences and cognitive learning styles include field dependence and independence as well as impulsivity and reflectivity. Cultural learning styles might include gesturing patterns, touching patterns, and use of humor.

9. Gender, social class, religion, race, ethnicity, geographic region, exceptionalities, and nationality are to be considered when making classroom decisions. Honoring Thanksgiving, a holiday that is celebrated by one group, of which many of the students at Emma Lazarus Elementary School are not members, might be inappropriate. Perhaps a program honoring thanksgiving or harvest celebrations of many groups might be a way to involve everyone.

10. While behavior differences may be greater within groups than between them, research shows that gesturing and touching patterns as well as the use of humor and joking influence the ways in which students approach learning tasks.

11. This is a question that requires personal beliefs about book banning; however, consider one side of the argument -- that offensive books, those that teach prejudice and hate, should not be part of a school's library collection -- and then the other -- that the Constitution of the United States allows for freedom of speech, regardless of how offensive that speech, or book might be.

SELF-ASSESSMENT ANSWERS   Chapter 5

1. d. Feeling anxious when a teacher announces a pop quiz is a learned response. This reaction may be unconscious or involuntary, but it is learned nonetheless. The student associates pop quiz with a less than enjoyable circumstance over which she/he has little control.

2. Animals exhibiting conditioned responses when they hear a tone (e) is an example of classical conditioning. Animals using trial and error to learn to escape from a box (d) and animals learning to press a lever to get food (a) are examples of the Law of Effect and of operant conditioning. Observing the behavior of children after they had seen films in which adults acted aggressively (b) is an example of observational learning.

3. a. Primary reinforcer satisfy basic human needs. Some examples are food, water, security, warmth, and sex.

4. The Premack principles states that activities less desired by learners can be increased by linking them to more desired activities. Two examples of the Premack principle include: 1) giving students computer game time when their work is finished; and 2) extending recess time if students' behavior is exemplary prior to recess.

5. Writing "I will not talk" 500 times (a) is most probably an example of punishment. Students who finish this work will not be assigned extra homework tonight (b) is most probably an example of negative reinforcement; however, be careful about calling learning (homework) undesired. Saying "Good job, class" (c) is most likely an example of positive reinforcement.

6. a.   Attention, retention, reproduction, and motivation are observational learning phases.

7. c.   Vicarious learning is observing the consequence of others' behavior. Meichenbaum's model for cognitive behavior modification centers on the individual asking himself/herself questions such as, "What is my problem? What is my plan? How did I do?"

8. Ms. Esteban is trying to teach her class to raise their hands and wait to be called on, yet she reinforces (pays attention to) students who do not exhibit these behaviors. For example, she calls on Rebecca even thought she shouts out her response before being called on by the teacher. Ms. Esteban attempts to ignore Rebecca's inappropriate behavior (extinction), but fails to do so.

9. Punishments, like reprimands or loss of privileges, do not work well with students, according to behavioral theorists. Most classroom behaviors can be managed through the use reinforcers. This requires paying attention to desired behaviors and ignoring (unless safety is an issue) inappropriate ones. Many teachers use punishment because, whether we like it or not, it is a part of our schools, communities, and value system.

10. B.F. Skinner would wait for the student to exhibit appropriate behaviors, then reinforce them. He might contract with the student by giving her or him something desired in exchange for not "acting out." Albert Bandura would have the student watch non-acting out behaviors, make sure the student can retain and physically demonstrate what was observed, and then provide some motivation for acting appropriately.

SELF-ASSESSMENT ANSWERS   Chapter 6

1. e. The sensory register is the component of the memory system where information is received and held for very short periods of time. It has two important educational implications. First, people must pay attention to information if they are to retain it and secondly, it takes time to bring all the information seen in a moment into consciousness.

2. The memory component from which information is most easily lost (a) is the sensory register. The component in which enormous amounts of general information can be stored (b) is semantic memory. The component that processes new information and also old information that has been brought to consciousness (c) is short term or working memory. The storage system in which memories of experiences can be stored (d) is episodic memory.

3. a. Sperling's research demonstrated that when people tried to recall all twelve letters in his experiment, the time it took them to do so apparently exceeded the amount of time the letters lasted in their sensory registers, so they lost some of the letters.

4. retroactive, proactive. Retroactive inhibition is the decreased ability to recall previously learned information caused by learning of new information. Proactive inhibition is the decreased ability to learn new information because of interference of present knowledge.

5. Overlearning, automaticity, and enactment support the claim that "practice makes perfect" while massed practice does not support it.

6. Memorizing the names of the world's continents in order by size (a) is an example of serial learning. Memorizing the names, functions, and locations of the major organs in the human body (c) is an example of free recall learning. Learning that a group of geese is a gaggle (d) is an example of paired-associate learning.

7. School and life in general would most likely be confusing. One important function of the information processing system is that it helps us attend to important information in our environments while ignoring or paying less attention to unimportant information.

8. It seems that all students -- low achievers, disadvantaged students, and high achievers would benefit from training in memory strategies.

SELF-ASSESSMENT ANSWERS   Chapter 7

1. d. Learner control does not describe effective instruction. The other terms listed demonstrate the interaction between the student and the teacher.

2. g, f, c, b, e, a, d. The seven steps in a direct instruction lesson would be in the following order: g) State learning objective and orient students to lesson; f) Review prerequisites; c) Present new material; b) Conduct learning probes; e) Provide independent practice; a) Assess performance and provide feedback; d) Provide distributed practice and review.

3. d. Direct instruction methods do not work well in the teaching of critical thinking skills, according to the research. Direct instruction is particularly appropriate in teaching a well-defined body of information or skills that all students must master. It is less appropriate when exploration, discovery, and open-ended objectives are the object of instruction.

4. a. Research indicates that low achievers should have as much time to respond as high achievers. Research has also found that teachers tend to give up too rapidly on students whom they perceive to be low achievers and not give them the same amount of wait time.

5. b. Transfer of learning is the application of knowledge acquired in one situation to new situations. Students having a knowledge of geometry should be better prepared to solve a perspectives problem in art.

6. Ms. Logan's approach is effective for gaining students attention and motivating them to test theories through exploration. A disadvantage to this discovery approach is that students may not discover the concept. Inquiry training has similar advantages and disadvantages. Direct instruction insures that students will be exposed to correct, complete concepts, however, they have little control over the learning environment. Mastery learning has similar advantages and disadvantages.

7. During a whole-class discussion, the teacher plays the role of moderator. They guide the discussion and help the class avoid dead ends, but ideas are drawn from students. Rules about how to deal with students who are quiet, or who talk too much or interrupt, should be determined and explained to students before the discussion begins.

SELF-ASSESSMENT ANSWERS   Chapter 8

1. c. In mediated learning the teacher guides instruction so that students will master and internalize the skills that permit higher cognitive functioning.

2. c. Constructivist approaches to teaching emphasize top-down rather than bottom-up instruction. The term top-down means that students begin with complex problems to solve and then work out or discover the basic skills required.

3. Self-regulated learning means that students have a say in what and how they will learn, at least to a degree. Science projects are an example of self-regulate learning. Scaffolding provides support for learning and problem solving, which could include clues, reminders, encouragement, breaking the problem down into steps, or providing an example. Discovery learning gives students opportunities to learning on their own through active involvement with concepts and principles. Experiments are often discovery learning activities.

4. d. Research suggests that cooperative learning programs are not effective where students are grouped together by ability. Mixed-ability grouping seems to have better results.

5. c. Functional fixedness is a block to solving problems that is caused by an inability to see new uses for familiar objects or ideas.

6. A constructivist view of learning suggests that students learn by building their own knowledge or understanding of the world. In the opening scenario, students are asked to discover the formula for computing the volume of a cylinder. They are given the tools needed to solve the problem, but not the formula. Through experimentation, the students arrive at the solution.

7. The role of a teacher in a discovery lesson is that of facilitator. The teacher can teach in ways that make information meaningful and relevant to students, by giving them opportunities to discover or apply ideas themselves, and by teaching students to be aware of and consciously use their own strategies for learning. A disadvantage of discovery learning might be that some ideas are to "discovered", leaving some students with fragmented knowledge or misconceptions.

8. Students sometimes have a problem see some unconventional problem solving strategies. Teachers can facilitate problem solving by assisting students in identifying goals, procedures, and roadblocks.

SELF-AWARENESS ANSWERS   Chapter 9

1. e. Quality of instruction, appropriate levels of instruction, incentive, and time, all components of the QAIT model are considered to be alterable elements that are necessary for instruction to be effective.

2. a. aptitude; b. opportunity; c. perseverance; d. ability to understand; e. quality of instruction.

3. Within-class ability grouping may be preferable to between-class ability grouping because it is most likely based on a teacher's assessment of what students need rather than standardized tests, it provides role models for lower achieving students, and it does not pull students away from the group with whom they identify.

4. d. Mastery learning allows learning time to vary while keeping level of achievement consistent. This provides for student differences. The basic idea behind mastery learning is to make sure that all students have learned a particular skill to a preestablished level of mastery before moving on to the next skill.

5. a. Norm-referenced tests that compare students to each other are not central features of mastery learning. In mastery learning the goal is to have the student compete with himself/herself in terms of his/her mastery of the material.

6. a. Tutorial programs are computer programs that teach lessons by varying their content and pace according to the student's responses. They are intended to teach new material. The best tutorial programs come close to mimicking a patient human tutor.

7. b. Special education programs in comparison to the other programs indicated do not target students from poor or disadvantaged backgrounds. These kind of programs cut across all socioeconomic barriers. The other programs listed in the answers focus on low-income and disadvantaged students.

8. Mr. Arbuthnot begins the lesson on long division by testing students' prior knowledge. He uses the results to group high achieving students with students who need a review of subtraction and multiplication facts. He monitors students' understanding of the new material throughout the lesson, reviewing when necessary.

9. Traditional classrooms can impede the use of mastery learning because they are based on time (the amount of information a student can learn during a unit, a quarter, a semester, a year) rather than the learning itself (learning all the information, regardless of he time it takes).

10. One factor that would make a peer tutoring program effective would be to use high school students as tutors for the middle school students. A second factor would be to adequately train and monitor the tutors.

SELF-ASSESSMENT AWARENESS   Chapter 10

1. e. physiological; f. safety; b. belongingness and love; c. self-esteem; d. need to know and understand; a. aesthetic; g. self-actualization.

2. a. attribution; b. cognitive dissonance; c. expectancy.

3. c. A student with an internal locus of control is one who believes that success or failure is due to his or her own efforts or abilities.

4. b. The internal-unstable falls into the category. Ability and effort attributions are internal to the individual. Although task difficulty is essentially a stable characteristic, the teacher wants the students to try harder regardless of ability level or task difficulty. Luck is unstable and unpredicatable.

5. b. A student who tends to choose either very easy or very hard tasks would most likely be avoiding failure. When students succeed, they would like to believe that it was because they are smart, not because they were lucky or because the task was easy. Students who fail would like to believe that they had bad luck, which allows for the possibility of succeeding next time.

6. a. Students who are motivationally oriented toward learning goals would be more interested in taking a challenging course. Their interest in the topic becomes a driving force because of the opportunity to make themselves more knowledgeable regardless of the difficulty of the material.

7. c. The main idea underlying the individual Learning Expectations (ILE) model is grading on the basis of improvement. With the ILE model students are recognized for doing better than they have done in the past, for steadily increasing performance until they are producing excellent work all the time.

8. a. cooperative; b. individualized; c. competitive.

9. In a math class, students might conduct polls about issues that are important to them, then statistically analyze the data. In a science class, students might work with local officials conducting studies on river quality (or other environments of concern). In an English class, students might write position papers, then submit them as editorials or letters to the editor at a local paper. In a language class, students might use the Internet to communicate with students in a foreign country.

10. Skinner would say that the student is motivated to get good grades because she or he has been or wants to be rewarded for doing so. Maslow would say that the student is motivated to get good grades because he or she has an underlying need to know and understand the world.

11. Grading on improvement might tell students who have not done well in the past to feel they still have an opportunity to be successful; however, grading on improvement might be an inaccurate representation of what students actually know. Additionally, it hurts high achieving students because they have less room to improve.

SELF-ASSESSMENT ANSWERS   Chapter 11

1. c. Engaged time, or time on-task, the number of minutes actually spent learning, is the time measure that is most frequently found to contribute to learning.

2. d. Group alerting refers to questioning strategies that are designed to keep all students on their toes during a lecture or discussion. If the teacher in the example given had asked the question of the entire class before calling on Cassandra, then Kounin's recommendation would have been followed.

3. a. withitness; b. group alerting; c. overlapping; d. accountability

4. c. nonverbal cues; d. verbal reminders; a. repeated reminders; b. consequence

5. a. peer attention; b. release from frustration; c. teacher attention

6. d. Identify target behavior and its reinforcer; b. Establish a baseline for target behavior; a. Select and use reinforcers and, if necessary, punishers; c. Phase out reinforcement.

7. c. Behavioral learning theory suggests that teachers use programs and strategies based on observation of correct behavior and rewards.

8. While they can be effective management tools, behavior modification techniques can be misuesed to humiliate, manipulate, overcontrol, incorrectly motivate and inappropriately punish students.

9. There could be many reasons why Gloria was late to class. Perhaps she was finishing a test in the previous class or she was called to the office. How Gloria's lateness might be handle if it happened again would depend, once again, on her reason for being late. From information gathered on moral development, we know that tenth grade students can consider the intentions of the rule breaker and context in which the rule was broken, although Mark was upset that Gloria was not asked to see Ms. Cavalho after school. Younger children might say that rules are rules, never to be broken, regardless of circumstances.

10. Research first suggests that teachers should use reinforcers to increase desired behaviors rather than punishers to decrease undesired ones. Punishers should only be used as the last option and should involve a loss of privilege(s), but never physical punishment.

11. Speaking out of turn is a minor infraction and should be ignored or stopped with a soft reprimand. Teasing another student might best be handled by speaking privately with the teaser. Modeling and praising of appropriate relationship behaviors would help. shoving another student on the playground is a serious safety issues that calls for intervention.

SELF-ASSESSMENT ANSWERS   Chapter 12

1. The terms handicap and disability are not interchangeable. A disability is a functional limitation a person has that interfers with her or his physical or cognitive abilities. A handicap is a condition imposed on a person with disabilities by society, the physical environment, or the person's attitude.

2. c. A student with mental retardation who has an IQ between 50 and 75 is considered to mildly retarded according to the American Association on Mental Retardation.

3. a. language disorder; b. speech disorder; c. specific learning disability; d. emotional disorder.

4. acceleration and enrichment. Acceleration programs offer rapid promotion through advanced studies for students who are gifted or talented. Enrichment programs presents assignments or activities which are designed to broaden or deepen the knowledge of students who master classroom lessons quickly.

5. 1. general education classroom; 2. resource room; 3. part time mainstreaming; 4. self-contained special education classroom.

6. 1. referral for evaluation; 2. placement; 3. testing and assessment; 4. signed parental approval of the IEP.

7. Effective teaching of mainstreamed students with special needs in general education classrooms involves cooperative learning, computerized instruction, buddy systems, peer tutoring, consultation with special education specialists, and team teaching.

8. Pleasantville staff believe that all children can learn and that it is their responsibility to teach them. The program is organized to identify students' strengths as well as problems and to provide the best program it can for each child.

9. Sometimes students with disabilities need extra time with the teacher, who is perhaps already overburdened with a large class size and inadequate support services. Using peer tutors or buddies could help to lessen this problem.

10. Tests used to determine eligibility for special services may not be appropriate for students who belong to a minority group. Minority group students are over represented in impoverished groups, which might mean they come from communities that cannot afford adequate educational facilities and programs.

SELF-ASSESSMENT ANSWERS   Chapter 13

1. b. The student being able to correctly solve 10 out of 12 division problems involving up to two-digit numbers satisfies the measurable criteria proposed by Mager. Mager, whose work began the behavioral objectives movement, described objectives as having three parts: performance, conditions, and criteria.

2. d. Analysis objectives involve having students see the underlying structure of complex information or ideas.

3. c. Behavior content matrix is a chart that classifies lesson objectives according to cognitive level. Using a behavior content matrix in setting objectives forces you to consider objectives above the knowledge and comprehension levels.

4. Evaluations provide students with feedback about their work, assist teachers in making instructional decisions, inform parents as to how their child is doing, provide information for selection into certain programs, assure accountability, and provide incentives for achievement.

5. c. Gronlund's principles of achievement testing does not indicate that tests should have items of the objective type. Gronlund's first principle, that achievement tests should measure well-specified objectives, is an important guide to the content of any achievement test.

6. a. summative; b. criterion-referenced; c. formative; d. norm-references.

7. a. The purpose of devising a table of specifications in testing is to indicate the types of learning to be assessed for different instructional objectives.

8. d. A recommendation in constructing multiple-choice items is making distractors plausible. The distractors (the wrong choices) must look plausible to the uninformed student. In other words, their wording and form must not identify them readily as bad answers.

9. Mr. Sullivan is an effective teacher. He gains students' interest by recalling anecdotes about the Civil War. He teacher history in math lessons (interrelating themes across the curriculum). He makes history come alive for his students. However, Mr. Sullivan is an ineffective evaluator. He teaches one thing, then tests another. Defining the outcomes he wants, planning lessons to address the outcomes, then testing to determine whether students have learned the outcomes would make Mr. Sullivan an effective evaluator.

10. Both objective and subjective assessments of student work are useful in making educational decisions; however, research about the reliability of portfolio assessment is disappointing because different raters have given very different ratings on the same portfolio.

11. Parents are capable of understanding both norm-references and criterion-referenced grading. Parents of young children often see their students assessed achievement of skills. Parents of older children and adolescents often look for comparisons of their son or daughter with others, especially on standardized tests.

SELF-ASSESSMENT ANSWERS   Chapter 14

1. c. Aptitude tests are designed to predict future performance. It is meant to predict the ability of students to learn or perform particular types of tasks rather than to measure how much the students have already learned.

2. b. Since the national mean on the standardized test is 50 and the percentile of the student's reported score is also 50, the correct response is b.

3. c. The first-period class has a larger standard deviation. Standard deviation is a statistical measure of the degree of dispersion in a distribution of scores.

4. c. It can be assumed that the student has scored as well on the test as the average ninth-grader, since she earned the equivalent of 9.4, which may be interpreted as ninth grade, fourth month.

5. d. Reliability is a measure of the consistency of test scored obtained from the same students at different times. In theory, if a student were to take the same test twice, he or she should obtain the same score both times. Generally, the longer the test and the greater the range of items, the greater the reliability.

6. c. Over the years the chronological age/mental age comparison has been dropped, and IQ is now defined as having a mean of 100 and a standard deviation of 15. Most scores fall near the mean, with small numbers of scores extending well above and below the mean.

7. a. The validity of a test refers to whether the test provides the type of information desired. Tests that contain cultural or gender bias lack validity.

8. Validity and reliability do not refer to tests. Instead they refer to test results. Valid test results measure some aspect of learning consistently over time. Test results can be consistent over time without measuring what is intended to be measured.

9. It is part of a teacher's job to report test results to parents. Hopefully, Ms. Tranh works at a school that provides her with information on how to interpret scores (through workshops, inservices, or staff development activities). If Mr. or Mrs. McKay became upset with the explanations of their daughter's scores, Ms. Tranh should ask them to meet with the school counselor, school psychologist, or other support person who has been specially trained in standardized assessment analysis.

10. Being graded on the curve shows how a student is achieving in relationship to his or her peers while sometimes promoting unfair and artificial competition among students. Cooperative group grades encourage students to work as a team toward the success of all; however, high achieving students are penalized if individual grades are averaged. Criterion-reference grading allows students to work toward some standard that is determined ahead of time, but, at the same time, sets a goal that might not be reached by anyone.

11. An individual who has a stanine score of 5 on a standardized achievement test would be at the 50th percentile, meaning half the test takers scored above and half scored below.